FAREWELL TO KOSOVO

*For Becca & Frank
How wonderful it is to see you
again after so many years...*

*March 10, 2013
LA*

OMER ERTUR

osertur@yahoo.com
www.omertur.com

Farewell to Kosovo
by Omer Ertur

Copyright © February 2012 Omer Ertur
All Rights Reserved

ISBN-13: 978-1470091538
ISBN-10: 1470091534

Library of Congress Control Number: 2012903120
CreateSpace Independent Publishing Platform
North Charleston, South Carolina

The first edition published in 2004 under the title
Soul Mates: Kosovo 1910 in *November 2003* ISBN 0-9741253-0-X

The Turkish edition published under the title
Can Yoldaslari:Kosova 1910 in November 2003, ISBN 0-9741253-1-6

REVIEWS

"Now we, the Turks, have become the enemy in our own country," laments a refugee leading a convoy of villagers fleeing the advancing Serbian army. Cries similar to this one spoken by a character in Omer Ertur's stunning and very personal novel, *Farewell to Kosovo*, have been heard too often during the series of wars that have raged through the Balkans in the last century. Ertur knows this, for not only has he been to Kosovo, but it is where his mother was born and where his grandfather fought during the dying days of the Ottoman Empire. Originally published in 2004 under the title *Soul Mates: Kosovo 1910*, Ertur's book is a fictionalized recollection of the stories he heard from his mother and grandmother. Set during the Turkish retreat from the Balkans in January of 1910, it is a novelized account of his grandfather's fight and his grandmother's flight, fleshed out with a second, imaginative storyline involving a young man from their village who finds himself fighting first on one side and then on the other in what is both an ethnic and a civil war. And what a cruel war it is, with Serbian soldiers conducting bayonet practice on prisoners (it "saves bullets and gets the new recruits ready for battle," chortles their officer) and raping young women one night, only to slit their throats in the morning. Both sides, as one of Ertur's characters sighs, are guilty of such atrocities, having convinced themselves that "these targets are not human beings; they are just enemies to be destroyed." This is not Ertur's first book, but it is the most personal of the three he has published. Like *Bones in the Nile*, about the Sudan campaign of 1884-1885, and *A Prelude to Gallipoli: The Battle of Broken Hill 1915*, this is a war novel that recounts not only the experiences of men in battle, but also what it does to their humanity. While Ertur admits that most of what he has put down in the 257 pages of his book is fiction, it is based on solid research, including oral histories received from a very personal primary source—his grandmother. And as a

United Nations officer in 1999, Ertur had the opportunity to walk the very ground where his grandparents' story played out, and this is reflected in the authenticity with which he depicts the battlegrounds and villages, and the people who fought and fled from there. Ertur's characters are written with a grace and depth that bring them to life as vividly as if they are standing before the reader on a screen or stage. There is a *Dr. Zhivago* feel to the book, and not just because this and Pasternak's work are set in the same era. *Farewell to Kosovo* has the same kind of intensity and validity found in Pasternak's tale of people trying to escape from the maelstrom of an empire in collapse, yet it has the added power of being based on the lives of members of the author's family. Those family members are presented both in print and in photos by Ertur. Eight pages from a family album are included with the text, one of which also serves as the cover image. The fire, intensity, and determination in the eyes of his grandparents in that picture are brilliantly captured in Ertur's prose.

Clarion Review

"Reading Farewell to Kosovo, with its extraordinary characters and historic scenes, I fully empathized with the sufferings of the uprooted Muslims of Kosovo at the beginning of twentieth century. While reading this book, I felt aches of sadness in my heart for the anguish it described, and, at the same time, I felt flutters of pleasure for the survivors. I kept asking myself, 'Why do we human beings inflict so much suffering against each other?' I say shame on those who re-enacted bloody atrocities similar to those in Kosovo almost eighty years after the incidents that occurred at the beginning of the twentieth century. Similarly, I also say shame on those who silently participated in the massacres as they watched the ongoing atrocities under their blue helmets as part of the UN peace-keeping force. Contrary to the political circumstances of the early twentieth century, which did not recognize the existence of human rights, recent conflicts in Kosovo have occurred in defiance of human rights principles established by the United Nations. That has prompted me to ask, 'In order to benefit from these rights, do victims have to be members of a particular nationality?' My belief is that, without a sense of humanity, one cannot believe in human rights, and, without enforceable human rights, the concept of humanity has no meaning at all. Now is the time for all of us to become aware of the relationship between a sense of global humanity and human rights. We should do what is necessary to establish a set of enforceable human rights that will be applied equally to all humanity. If we can reach such a valuable goal in the beginning of the twenty-first century, we should all celebrate. This historical novel is a must for readers who seek a better understanding of the historical precedents that relate to the ethnic cleansing that occurred recently in Kosovo and the Balkans."

Yahya Akkurt,
Former Turkish Ambassador to Vietnam

"By getting to know and following the protagonist of this moving story through the pages of this most personal intimate insight into history, I have gained a deeper understanding of the many tragic conflicts that sadly continue today to affect the lives of thousands of innocent human beings. Focusing on the suffering of the Muslims in South-Eastern Europe, particularly in Kosovo and Macedonia, has brought me closer to a better conceptualization of the circumstances, and made me realize how little has really changed in the region and how far we still are from achieving stability, peace, harmony, and above all, respect for our cultural and religious diversity."

Rosamaria Durand,
UNESCO, Paris, France

"The reader is captivated by the weaving of personal and human stories into the overarching descriptions of warring factions on the verge of victory and retreat. The story reveals as much about individual courage as it does the difficult decisions and painful consequences involved in any military campaign. The author's detailed knowledge of the area and the time period -- and of course his obvious passion for the subject matter -- results in an unforgettable reading experience that is part history lesson and part love story."

Kathleen Palmer, JD.
Newport, Oregon, USA

"The action-filled scenarios in this story drove my feelings to the highest notes: from happiness to pain, from anger to sympathy, from tension to relief. I am impressed by the author's penmanship and thankful for the chance to learn about the ethnic conflicts that happened in the Balkans almost a century ago. I think *Farewell to Kosovo* would make a great movie."

Do Thi Thu Ha,
UNFPA, Hanoi, Vietnam

FOREWORD

This family novel is a fictionalized recollection of the stories I heard during my childhood from my grandmother Servet, my parents, my uncles and aunts, and many close and distant relatives. With the exception of my maternal grandparents, Avni and Servet, and their five children, including my mother Bedia, all the characters in the story are fictional. All of the cities, towns, and geographical locations mentioned in the story are real. For ease of reading, the modern names of places have been used rather than the old Ottoman names. The basic plot of the story is based on certain historical facts and events as well as on word-of-mouth stories from relatives and friends. As indicated in the introductory section (the prologue), my official visit to Kosovo in July 1999 as a United Nations officer was the beginning of a mystical travel through time to the era of my grandparents.

My grandparents' story, revealed through my imagination, is an eternal gift to their present-day descendants: their children and grandchildren. My grandmother's wonderful, kindred spirit has guided my efforts to inhabit the times of her youth. Though I never had the opportunity to meet my grandfather, I felt his presence in my mind leading me through the turmoil of life-threatening battles as he awaited the birth of his first child. My grandparents and my children represent generations almost a century apart. From the beginning of the twentieth century to the end, my grandparents' and parents' generations lived through tremendous hardships and sensational social changes. In remembering the lives of my parents and grandparents and looking deeply into the lives of my own children, I now realize that loyalty and trust remain the essential ingredients of all relationships.

May the Lord grant eternal peace to Lieutenant Avni and his soul mate Servet, and to my parents, Bedia and her soul mate Arif, who raised me with an abundance of love and devotion. Through my maternal grandparents' spiritual presence in my heart, I was able to reach deeply into the recent past to write this story for all who descended from these two unique individuals. The story of these two exceptional characters as soul mates is an account of survival against all odds and victory over daunting hardships achieved through love, courage, and loyalty. This family novel is a memorial to my beloved grandparents and a legacy to my children, Sufi and Adam.

Omer Ertur
November 2001
Hanoi, Vietnam

Acknowledgements

During the summer of 1999, I was given the opportunity to visit Kosovo as a United Nations official. Being in Kosovo right after the bloody conflicts between the local Serbian population and the Kosovo Albanians reminded me of stories I had heard from my grandmother during my childhood. Being in my mother's birthplace -- where my grandparents had lived almost a century ago -- compelled me to connect with my familial past and write the story of my grandparents. I would, therefore, like to express my sincere gratitude to Dr. Nafis Sadik, former executive director of the United Nations Population Fund (UNFPA), for selecting me for the Kosovo assignment. Her personal trust and professional confidence in me gave me the chance to become a member of the United Nations team in Kosovo.

In preparing this family novel, I was helped by many people. I am particularly grateful to all of the family members -- uncles, aunts, cousins, nieces and nephews, and many in-laws -- who, over the years, told me many stories about my grandparents. In particular, my sisters, Sevim Knowlton and Sumer Curtis, added substantially to my understanding of our grandparents' lives by telling me the stories they had heard from family elders before I was born.

I would also like to express my special appreciation to friends and family members who helped me with editorial corrections and idiomatic expressions that improved the flow of the complicated plot. Kathleen Ann Palmer, my friend of many years and mother of our son, Adam, and loving stepmother to my daughter, Sufi, has greatly contributed to the quality of my sentence structure over many hours of editorial corrections. A great friend and colleague, Rosamaria Durand of UNESCO, through her suggestions about character relationships and engaging schemes, has enriched the intricate plot of the story. Another trusted friend of many years, Sheila Macrae of UNFPA, edited the final draft for corrections in the proper usage of prepositions. A loyal and considerate friend, Do Thi Thu Ha of UNFPA-Vietnam gave many hours of her valuable personal time proofreading the earlier drafts. A respected friend and the Turkish Ambassador to Viet Nam, Yahya Akkurt, and my favorite nephew, Frederick Curtis, read the manuscript and provided me with many sensible and useful suggestions. Finally, two professional colleagues, Mr. Trieu Anh and Mr. Tom Greenwood proofread the final manuscript before its first printing. For the second printing of *Soul Mates* under its new title *Farewell to Kosovo*, I would like to express my special thanks to the members of my CreateSpace team for their exceptional publication advice and technical assistance. I also would like to extend my sincere gratitude to Julia Harte, Yahya Akkurt, and my son, Adam Ertur for their excellent editorial contributions that made my family story a pleasant read.

Omer Ertur
February 2012
Istanbul, Turkey

PROLOGUE
KOSOVO
1999

August 1999: Arrival in Kosovo

It was exactly noon when the plane landed on the tarmac at the Skopje airport. As I walked off the plane, I noticed how gray and gloomy the sky was. Descending the stairway, I noticed many people on the landing gazing at the sky. Gripping the railings, I looked up to see what was going on: a solar eclipse, my first ever! In the darkened sky, the sun and moon appeared in unison: a dark circle surrounded by a ring of orange sunlight. There was an eerie atmosphere of quiet and calm, as if time were standing still. Wondering if the eclipse portended good or evil, I proceeded to the terminal. After the usual immigration and customs formalities, I found the person I was supposed to meet outside the terminal. He stood tall amid the crowd: a dark and very thin man, thirty-something, holding a large "United Nations" placard on which my last name was misspelled. After quick introductions in English, I shook Mohsen's hand. He was the senior driver of the temporary office that had been set up by the team from the United Nations office in Albania. Under the dark and gloomy sky of the eclipse, we walked silently toward a vehicle with large UN logos affixed to both sides.

Getting in the driver's seat, Mohsen spoke English with a heavy accent. "If you don't mind, sir," he said, "I've got to stop by the United Nations Skopje office to pick up the diplomatic mail."

We started to drive toward Skopje. This charming Macedonian city was full of beautiful buildings that had been built during Ottoman rule. I was particularly enchanted by Skopje's unique urban skyline, which was full of mosques and minarets of various sizes and shapes. There were several domed bath-houses intermingled with ancient Greco-Roman structures and beautiful old churches. This wonderful architectural diversity illustrated the historical and cultural complexities of this captivating Balkan town. I was pleasantly surprised by how much this historic place resembled many of the Western Anatolian cities that I had visited during my youth in Turkey.

After a quick stop to get the diplomatic pouch from the UN office, we drove toward the Macedonia-Kosovo border. As the driver maneuvered the vehicle through the winding, narrow streets of the city center, I had a vision of my grandparents strolling down the cobblestone streets of Skopje almost a century earlier. Later, when we left the outskirts of the town behind, I glanced back at the fascinating silhouette of Skopje, its multiple domes and minarets reflecting a forgotten past buried deep within today's uneasy realities. I closed my eyes and imagined my grandparents departing from Macedonia for Kosovo on a horse-drawn wagon.

When we were about to reach the border, the driver loudly uttered a long and incomprehensible Albanian oath. He shyly glanced at me and explained, "The usual traffic jam at the border!"

He was referring to the long lines of armored military vehicles, occasional tanks, and numerous supply trucks loaded with emergency food and medicine intended for Kosovo. After a while, the traffic came to a complete stop.

Mohsen, turning off the engine, asked me if I was Turkish. I nodded and asked him, "Do you speak Turkish?" To my delighted surprise, he answered my question in fluent Turkish.

While waiting for two hours at the border, we talked about Kosovo and its recent armed political conflict with Serbia. As he explained the Kosovar-Albanian perspective of the bloody conflict, Mohsen presented me with a very emotional picture of the events that had taken place during the previous six months. He told me that he and his family had escaped from Pristina with little more than their lives, spending over three months in refugee camps along the Macedonian border.

Finally, after completing the lengthy border formalities, he started to drive speedily toward Pristina. I told Mohsen in Turkish that my mother had been born in a Kosovo town called Yeniova. Mohsen was visibly intrigued by this news. Holding the steering wheel with one hand, he reached out and touched my shoulder.

"You're an Albanian; you're my brother."

"Yes, I'm your brother in some ways, but not from my mother's side. My paternal grandfather was from the Albanian city of Tirana. That makes us brothers in more than the fact that my mother just happened to be born in Kosovo. By the way, where is Yeniova?"

Mohsen slowed the vehicle to a stop at the side of the road and turned toward me. Pointing to a range of mountains to my right, he answered, "It's now called Yanyevo. It's somewhere between those mountains. Shall we drive there now?"

Looking in the direction he pointed, I observed a long stretch of southern Kosovo plains. The town of Yanyevo was located in the distant range of green hills.

I answered, "Not now, but soon, definitely very soon."

Mohsen, apparently confused about my family background, shyly asked me to explain how my mother happened to be born in Yanyevo.

"My dear brother Mohsen," I replied. "It's a long story. I'll tell you all about it when we visit Yanyevo."

The Visit to Yanyevo

A few weeks later, one early morning while on route to an official meeting in the northern city of Mitrovica, Mohsen and I took a detour and stopped at Yanyevo. After a quick cup of tea in a local coffeehouse directly across from the central mosque, I decided to take a solitary walk through the streets of Yanyevo to experience some familial history and to have a mental journey back to the beginning of the year 1910, when my mother was born in this charming little town. To etch this unique moment into my memory, I stood in the middle of the central square and deliberately focused my vision on the hillsides surrounding the town. Slowly turning on my heels, much like a whirling dervish, I shifted my focus from the distant hills to the closer scenery near the town square. Lush green, rolling hills encircled a group of gardens and houses with red-tiled roofs. A web of cobblestone pathways descended down the hillsides and merged with dense clusters of old wooden houses. A collection of brick buildings surrounded an old church, and there were a few old mansions on the wide, hillside streets, which converged at the town square on the immediate periphery of the seventeenth-century mosque.

A hand suddenly touched my shoulder, startling me out of my reverie. A middle-aged man stood right next to me. He spoke in Turkish.

"Brother, your driver told me that your mother was born here. May I offer you some assistance?"

We stood in the middle of the square and talked for a long time. He told me that before the Balkan Wars, Yanyevo had been the main supply center for the Ottoman army regiments fighting in Kosovo and old Serbia. He mentioned that there was a large military hospital up the hillside, near the mosque.

Pointing to the rundown coffeehouse where I had enjoyed a cup of tea earlier, he said, "This coffeehouse was built after the big war. The old coffeehouse that was burned down during the war used to be in that same exact spot."

Appreciating this information, I thanked the man and asked him if the mosque was open. He replied that it was always open. I asked him to excuse me so that I could go to the mosque and perform a special prayer.

Alone in the old mosque, I completed the formal prayers. Then I sat on the large, beautiful Turkish carpet and silently prayed for the souls of my parents and long-departed grandparents. I thanked the Lord for this opportunity to see the birthplace of my mother.

When I left the mosque, I found the man sitting on the stone stairway outside the ablution area. He rose to his feet and said, "May the good Lord accept your prayers for the departed and grant them eternal peace."

I thanked the stranger for his kind words and asked if it was possible to visit the old church on the hillside above the mosque.

He answered with confidence, "No problem, the priest is a good friend of mine. I'll take you there; let's go."

As we walked toward the old Croatian Catholic church, I asked the stranger, "How do you know so much about the history of this town?"

"My brother," he said, "I am a Kosovo Albanian. I was born here. I've lived here all my life. My father and my grandfather told me all about the times of the Turks here in Kosovo. My grandfather was recruited to the Ottoman army in 1910 during the conflicts over the territories of old Serbia. He survived many bloody battles. When I was a child, he told me about the history of Kosovo. I heard so many times from my grandfather how the Turks fought valiantly to keep old Serbia and Kosovo within the Ottoman Empire, but to no avail. The Turks lost many battles, and one cold winter day in 1912, they left Kosovo for good."

I was intrigued by the detailed history he had presented. I asked, "The Turks left Yanyevo almost a century ago. How come you still speak fluent Turkish?"

"Most Albanian households in Kosovo speak three languages: Albanian, Serbo-Croatian, and Turkish."

I repeated the question, "But why do you continue to speak Turkish?"

With a broad smile, he answered, "We thought the Turks might come back one day." Affectionately grasping my shoulder, he continued, "And here you are!"

The Albanian man led me to the old Croatian Catholic church, where I was welcomed warmly by the head priest. He personally unlocked the grand, old wooden door of the church. I entered the beautifully ornamented and well-maintained two-hundred-year-old building. I asked the priest if I could climb up to the bell tower for a bird's-eye view of the town.

The priest responded that the stairs leading to the bell tower were hazardous and full of holes. "However," he added, "if I lead you up the old wooden stairs, you'll be safe."

Slowly and with carefully measured steps, we climbed the bell tower. From a wobbly wooden landing at the top, I glanced at the main church hall below, imagining the parish gatherings that had taken place for centuries during Sunday prayers.

As we reached the top of the bell tower, I informed the priest that I worked for the United Nations. In response, the priest commented that for centuries Albanians, Croats, and Serbians had coexisted peacefully in Yanyevo. In reference to the present conflict, he said, "Now, there are only a few Croats and Serbians remaining in Yanyevo. Most of them have moved to Serbia or to the newly established state of Croatia."

After a few more minutes of discussion about the situation in Kosovo, the priest excused himself and left me alone in the bell tower.

I was moved by the panoramic view I faced: a wonderful display of a mixture of new and old structures within a prolific landscape that was crisscrossed by a collection of worn-out cobblestone pathways leading to the recently paved road at the central square. This overwhelming view encouraged me to imagine how this charming little town must have appeared at the beginning of the twentieth century, when it was my grandparents' home.

I broke my reverie and descended the treacherous, squeaky stairs. The Albanian was patiently waiting for me outside the church. As we walked down the hill's winding pathway toward the town square, he asked if my driver and I would join him and his family for tea and breakfast at his home. Wanting to know more about the history of the town, I gratefully accepted the offer.

During breakfast, we talked about Yanyevo and our grandparents, who must have shared experiences of some sort in this little town, nestled among the high hills of central Kosovo. Before asking permission to leave, I commented, "My dear Albanian brother, we have been calling each other 'brother' since our acquaintance this morning. My name is Omer. What's yours?"

The Albanian answered, "I was named after my grandfather, whose name was Avni."

Suddenly feeling the inexplicable mystery of coincidences, I informed him that my grandfather's name was also Avni. I gave him a warm hug and thanked him for his time and generosity.

The driver and I boarded the vehicle to continue our journey to the town of Mitrovica in northwestern Kosovo. Within a few minutes, we reached the bottom of the valley. When we neared the junction that connected to the main road, Mohsen pointed out a couple small villages in close proximity to each other and said, "These are Serb villages."

Noticing that the road to those villages was blocked by a group of NATO soldiers, I asked Mohsen the reason.

He spoke without any expression on his face. "NATO first tried to protect us from the murderous Serbian attacks," he said pensively. "Now it protects them from us. It's tempting to get even with the Serbians after what they did to so many Kosovo Albanian families, but most of us are not trying to get even with them. We're not raised to seek hatred and revenge."

"Mohsen, are you telling me that there are no bad Albanians and no good Serbians?"

"Honestly sir, before answering your question, let me remind you that we didn't start this damned conflict. Yes, there are plenty of good Serbians. Let me give you an example: in order to save our lives, my family and I hid in the apartment of our Serbian upstairs neighbor. When the Serbian police came to look for us, they found our apartment empty. They came upstairs to question our Serbian neighbor, who told them that we'd left the city for Macedonia. Our Serbian neighbor knew that if the police found us, they would definitely kill me and my fourteen-year-old son. They would then expel the rest of the family to Macedonia. We stayed with this wonderful woman for two weeks. One rainy evening, we escaped and found our way to the refugee campgrounds in Macedonia."

I was intrigued by Mohsen's story. I wanted to know more. "What happened to your Serbian neighbor when Kosovo was liberated?" I asked.

"She moved to southern Serbia," he replied. "After she left Pristina, her apartment was ransacked. But I've been able to keep her apartment intact so that if she ever returns to Pristina she will have her home back."

Mitrovica 1999

Early in the afternoon, we finally reached Mitrovica. I noticed that the main street leading to the bridge over the river Sitnica, which separated the Serbian quarters from the Kosovo Albanian neighborhoods, was full of people. Mohsen told me that for some reason a group of local Albanians wanted to cross the bridge to attack the people in Serbian quarter. A large number of French soldiers were trying hard to keep the crowd under control. The mob, determined to cross the bridge at any cost, was pushing against the French soldiers who barricaded the bridge.

Mohsen pulled the car to the curb and parked it. For a while, we watched the ongoing skirmishes at the bridge.

I asked him, "Is it safe to leave the car?"

He nodded and opened the door to get out. He was suddenly surrounded by several French soldiers. After a few minutes of heated discussion, the driver returned to the car.

"We have to move the car across the street to the parking lot next to the community affairs building where the French soldiers are housed. For security reasons, they requested that we remain there until the rioting ends."

He got back in the car and drove to the lot where several UN vehicles were parked. Recognizing some of the people with whom I was to meet that afternoon, I exited the car and approached them. While speaking with my colleagues, I noticed Mohsen running toward the bridge where the crowd was still rioting against the well-armed French soldiers. Though I was concerned for my driver's safety, I also wanted to know more about the ongoing riot. I was sure that Mohsen would return with some explanations about the confrontation between the Albanian community and the French NATO soldiers.

Revenge and Retribution

My official meeting with several UN staff and civil society professionals had ended by early evening. The local community support group informed all of us at the meeting that, due to security concerns we would have to spend the night in the community center. An evening meal and makeshift bedrooms were being prepared for the representatives of the UN agencies and various international organizations.

I walked out of the building into the parking lot and strolled slowly toward the River Sitnica. I sat on a grassy knoll near the water. It was a warm, windy evening with a full moon glowing on the fast-flowing water. Across the river, bright yellow street-lights flickered off and on, reflecting rhythmically from the windows of the densely built Serbian quarter. This effect combined with the unsettling commotion of sparkling lights bouncing on the fast-moving waves of the river propelled me to meditate. For a long while, I calmly watched the river flow. When I gazed at the shoreline on the other side, I noticed several armed civilians pacing the pedestrian walkways.

Suddenly, out of nowhere, Mohsen appeared in front of me with a bottle of local beer in each hand. Handing me one of the bottles, he sat down to tell me about all that he had discovered while investigating the rioting near the bridge. After downing over half of his beer in one swig, he told me, in a low and subdued voice, why the local Albanians were so adamant about crossing the bridge.

"Five months ago, in one of those Kosovo Albanian enclaves inside the Serbian quarter, five armed Serbian men drove all the Albanian families out of their homes. They separated the men and executed them in front of their families, right there on the pavement. One by one, they shot each Albanian in the back of his head. That day, twenty-six Albanian men of all ages were slaughtered by five Serbians who had been their neighbors, with whom they had grown up and gone to school. The women and children who survived the bloody ordeal tried to tell the world about what had happened, but they were not completely believed until the discovery of the mass grave where the twenty-six men had been buried. The Mitrovica Albanian community now asks for revenge and retribution. A few days ago, four of the five men who committed this savage crime escaped from the local NATO prison. The local community believes that they were allowed to escape by the French soldiers. The people feel that justice will never be served, so they have taken matters into their own hands. They wanted to cross the bridge to get even with their former neighbors, but they were prevented from doing so today. Nevertheless, sentiment remains strong that one day justice will be served, an eye for an eye."

I thanked Mohsen for this disturbing explanation of the afternoon's riot. As he was about to leave, I wished him a pleasant evening, but then, remembering that I had promised him the story of my mother's birth in Kosovo, I asked him to stay a bit longer. Before commencing with the story, I stared sadly for a long time at the sparkling waves of the river. I wondered why, given how drastically the whole world appeared to have changed since the beginning of the twentieth century, the primeval emotions in these parts of the Balkans remained intact and so easily ignited. I closed my eyes and imagined the natural and social panorama as it had been almost a century earlier, when my grandfather served in Kosovo as an officer in the retreating Ottoman army. I let my mind slowly drift into the historical events and never-ending conflicts of the Balkans at the beginning of the twentieth century.

* * *

FAREWELL TO KOSOVO 1910

WINDS OF DESPAIR

December 31, 1909: Soul Mates in Yanyevo

In his house, which faced the town square of Yanyevo, Lieutenant Avni, a twenty-two year old Ottoman army officer, calmly walked toward the window and opened it wide. He wanted to see what was causing the noisy commotion in the main square at such an early hour. Looking out, he noticed that the town of Yanyevo was welcoming a new group of wounded soldiers. He recognized Doctor Nuri running down the hill from the medical compound and shouting instructions over his shoulder to the medics trying to catch up with him. Across from the mosque, several mule carts full of wounded soldiers were lining up. As with previous arrivals, many of the wounded soldiers had probably not survived the treacherous journey. Lieutenant Avni shook his head in frustration at how few orderlies were around to move the wounded soldiers to the medical compound.

After closing the window, he slowly turned toward Servet, his eighteen year old spouse, who sat on the bed staring at her swollen abdomen.

"Dear wife, remember what Doctor Nuri told you yesterday evening. Please, stop worrying. You may be wrong about when the baby is due."

Servet slowly raised her head to look at her husband.

"Do you have to go for another munitions delivery trip? Why can't you wait until I have the baby?"

Moving away from the window, Avni walked toward the bed and sat next to his pregnant wife. "Yes, soon I may have to go back to the front again. The army is retreating from southern Serbia into northern Kosovo. No reinforcements are expected to arrive from the regional army in Thrace. The Serbian nationalist army and the Albanian insurgents under Isa Boletin could make a sudden move into northern Kosovo. In order to hold onto the area, we have to effectively halt the enemy's advance. If we cannot, then the patients, the hospital staff, and the staff of the military supply unit in Yanyevo must be evacuated to Skopje."

Avni reached toward Servet and gently touched her face with his fingertips. "My sweet wife," he said pleadingly. "I wish I could stay. But it is not possible." As he stared into her beautiful blue eyes, he continued in a strong voice, "God willing, I'll return safely. Please, don't worry."

Servet, trying hard not to cry, answered, "If we evacuate, how will you find me?" Referring to her unborn child, she corrected herself: "I mean ... us?"

Avni got his feet to leave. "If it's God's will, we'll grow old together; if not, you'll be looked after. Now, let's not talk about this anymore."

As he stepped out of the house, Avni felt that he would have succumbed to Servet's pleas had he stayed another moment. Because of the military circumstances, it was not possible for him to remain in Yanyevo. After receiving another supply delivery order two months ago, he had decided to remain behind for a while to keep Servet calm. Then he had asked the security officer, Lieutenant Nihad, to take the supplies coming in from Macedonia on to Southern Serbia. Unfortunately, his stay had not lasted long; a week later he had been ordered by Colonel Husnu to leave immediately for the front to deliver an emergency shipment of guns and ammunition to the infantry troops. Before his sudden departure, he had sent Servet a short note of farewell with Jemal, the orderly for the families of the three staff officers in the supplies management unit. When Avni had returned to Yanyevo a week later, he found Servet furious with him for leaving her alone so abruptly.

Reaching the town square, Avni noticed that Jemal was helping the medical orderlies remove the dead from the carts. Bodies were loaded into large wagons to be taken to the burial site. Unfortunately, at this time of year, it was extremely hard to dig graves in the frozen ground. He remembered how hard it had been for him to agree with Lieutenant Nihad's suggestion that the dead be buried in groups to save time and effort.

He noted the growing number of bodies in the wagons and muttered, "Another big grave to dig!" As he walked toward the coffeehouse across the main square, he was thinking how matters of life and death had become entwined in his day-to-day responsibilities. Lately, because he had been exposed to so much death and suffering, he had become emotionally numb. Ruminating on the fact that he was about to become a father, he rationalized that he couldn't be emotionless and feel so much excitement at the same time. He was, however, deeply concerned about the dangers his family would face in his absence. He wanted to finalize the arrangements for Servet and the baby to be evacuated to a safer location as soon as possible.

Avni entered the crowded and noisy coffeehouse and tried to locate Colonel Husnu through the heavily smoke-filled room. He was alone in his usual corner, slowly sipping his Turkish coffee. The colonel appeared tired and unshaven. Avni pulled up a chair and sat across from him.

Colonel Husnu launched into a conversation without greeting the lieutenant. "Today, more casualties than usual have arrived, and more than half of them were dead. The rest have little chance of surviving. We are understaffed and low on medical supplies. Worst of all, more wounded soldiers are on their way."

After a few moments of silence, the colonel raised his head and looked at Avni. "Good morning, Lieutenant," he said. "Today I was hoping to receive an order from headquarters to withdraw to Skopje. However, I received just the opposite. We've been ordered to mobilize all able-bodied men to go to the front in northern Kosovo. Avni, you are in charge of mobilizing our share of troops and getting them to the front. In the meantime, orders or no orders, I'll make preparations for the evacuation of all patients, staff, and dependents to Skopje as soon as possible."

Avni felt both disturbed and relieved at the same time. "Colonel," he inquired, "when do you think the families will move to Skopje?"

Colonel Husnu slowly stood up from his chair and approached Avni. "Lieutenant," he said apprehensively. "I know you're worried about your wife. I hope she will give birth before the evacuation. A four-day trip on a mule cart would not be good for a pregnant woman. I pray to the Lord that you become a father before the journey takes place, but please understand that I cannot delay the evacuation. It has to take place when the circumstances are safe for travel. Let's hope for the best. Please, quickly gather all able-bodied men to move to the front under your orders. You will have to depart tomorrow. Report to me as soon as you know how many men you can gather."

Avni, feeling dizzy and sick to his stomach, hastily questioned his superior. "Colonel, where am I going to find physically fit men to take to the front?" he asked. "There are only a few who are in good enough condition to fight. Furthermore, if I take all the able-bodied men with me, then who will help you with the evacuation? Who will provide security coverage during the evacuation? You know that the defensive lines at the old Serbia front are broken. Several enemy insurgent units have moved ahead toward Pristina. Some of those units may circumvent the northern Kosovo defense front and block the road to Skopje. You need men to stay with the convoy to defend the wounded and the families."

Colonel Husnu looked straight into Avni's eyes and growled, "Lieutenant, you'll do what I've ordered you to do. First, you're to mobilize all remaining village men between fourteen and sixty years of age. You'll then gather any wounded soldiers who have recovered enough to return to the front. Also, prepare a list of the medical and supply unit staff that will join you in this mission. I may retain a few men from that list to assist me during the evacuation. The rest will go with you. When you complete the list, report to me immediately."

After Colonel Husnu walked away, Avni sat silently for a while. He was confused and concerned about the order he had just received; he could see no logic in sending more soldiers to the front to be slaughtered. The dismantling of the Sanjak Province defense lines in southern Serbia just a few months earlier left fresh memories in his mind. He had taken all the presumably recovered soldiers and more than half of the support staff, including a few untrained local recruits, to the Sanjak front with him. At the time, Avni had hoped that the enemy's advance could be stopped. Only a few of the soldiers he had taken to southern Serbia had returned to Yanyevo. The rest had been killed or captured. Now, he was again being asked to lead another suicide mission to the crumbling front northwest of Pristina. Worst of all, he was not at all sure if his family would be safe in Yanyevo or during the planned evacuation to Skopje.

To calm his nerves and upset stomach, Avni asked Mehmetali, the owner of the coffeehouse, to bring him a large cup of tea.

The Renegade's Father

With sadness deep in his heart and growing anger in his guts, Jemal pulled the last dead soldier from the cart. When he turned the corpse face up, he recognized Huseyin, the younger son of Mehmetali. Huseyin was one of the last-resort local recruits; he had turned seventeen just a few months before his conscription.

Struggling to control his emotions, Jemal shook his head and pondered. *How am I going to tell Mehmetali? If Lieutenant Avni is in the coffeehouse, I could ask him to deliver the bad news.*

Jemal, a short and stocky Anatolian soldier with a thick, well-maintained black mustache adorning a large bulbous nose and dark-brown eyes, decided against asking the lieutenant. He knew many local families were bitter about the lieutenant's last effort to recruit local men for the front. Some local Albanian families had resisted the recruitment effort; one staff sergeant had been badly wounded during a skirmish with the local Albanian families. From then on, Lieutenant Avni had personally handled the recruitment efforts. On many occasions, Mehmetali had joined the lieutenant in appealing to the Albanian families not to oppose or disturb the recruitment process. He felt obligated to give recruitment assistance to Lieutenant Avni because Mehmetali's older son, Burhan, had joined the enemy army one year earlier. Mehmetali was ashamed of what Burhan had done. Because of this shame, he had not resisted when his younger son, Huseyin, was recruited into the Ottoman army.

Jemal delivered the corpse-laden wagon to the burial area. Walking to the coffeehouse, he rehearsed how he would deliver the bad news to Mehmetali. He entered the crowded room as Mehmetali was serving a cup of tea to the lieutenant. After saluting, Jemal asked permission to speak.

Avni, sipping his tea, looked inquisitively at Jemal and asked him to sit down. "Jemal," he said. "I saw you assisting the orderlies with the incoming wounded. I am afraid you want to talk to me about what you've discovered. Go ahead, tell me."

"Mehmetali's younger son ..." Jemal could not complete the sentence.

Full of dread, Avni asked, "Wounded?"

"No, he is dead," Jemal replied in a subdued voice. "Sir, I would like to inform Mehmetali."

"You don't have to do that," replied Avni. "I will tell him myself. It won't be easy, but it is my responsibility. Go tell my wife that I may be late for dinner. Meet me in the officers' mess hall in one hour. Dismissed!"

Remaining in the coffeehouse, Avni drank his lukewarm tea and recalled the day Mehmetali had helped him calm down the irritated local Albanian families during the last recruitment effort. Mehmetali had told the Albanian families that he was going to let his younger son join the Sanjak defense force. Avni knew why Mehmetali had allowed Huseyin to go to the front; he wanted to clear his name because his older son, Burhan, had unexpectedly disappeared and joined a group of Albanian irregulars serving in the Serbian army.

Avni thought, *His older son is a traitor and now I have to deliver the bad news that his younger son is dead.*

He reluctantly called Mehmetali over to join him.

Jemal's World

Servet, waking up from her usual afternoon nap, lay in bed staring up at the whitewashed bedroom ceiling. She hoped she would give birth to her first child as soon as possible. Feeling insecure and apprehensive, she wished she were at home in Izmit at her parents' house. Suddenly, she heard Jemal calling her name. When she opened the door, she noticed how tired and worn-out he looked. For a man in his mid-twenties, Jemal appeared much older.

After learning that Avni might be late for dinner, Servet asked, "Jemal, what is going on out there?"

Sensing that it was not a good time to tell the truth, Jemal mumbled, "We received more wounded soldiers. Other than that, not much is happening."

Recognizing Jemal's uneasiness, Servet insisted. "Tell me then, why is the lieutenant not coming home in time for supper?"

Jemal, wishing she would stop questioning him, remained silent. Staring directly into Jemal's eyes, Servet told him to tell her the truth.

"Madam," he replied nervously, "please ask the lieutenant to explain what's going on."

He quickly excused himself and walked away from the house. As he entered the manure-scented stable, Jemal realized how secure and happy he felt being there. He slowly pulled the lieutenant's horse, Yagiz, out of the stable to get her ready for the following day's journey. While he brushed the horse, he softly sang his favorite traditional Anatolian song 'Yarim', meaning 'my beloved'. After three long years in the military, two of which had been spent in the Balkans, he was more than ready to go home. Desperately homesick, he thought of the beautiful open plains of Sivas, his hometown in central Anatolia, and recalled fond memories of horseback riding through the gentle valleys surrounding his village. Aisha, his wife, was sitting behind him and Selim, his three-year-old son, on the front of the saddle. Aisha was hugging him, her arms around his chest, sweetly whispering the words of their favorite song into his ear.

Jemal stopped brushing Yagiz and mournfully whispered to the horse, "Oh, my beautiful friend, you don't know how much I long to be with my loved ones. I wonder if I'll survive this coming military retreat and see my home again."

Home seemed so far away to Jemal, especially because he was aware of the dangers the next day would bring. As he gently stroked the soft, warm muzzle of Yagiz, he sang the last few notes of the sad Anatolian melody. He felt the gentle touch of snowflakes upon his forehead and thought how peaceful everything appeared during the calm of the snowfall. He raised his head to look at the cloud-covered hills surrounding the town and felt completely at peace. Remembering that he was supposed to meet with the lieutenant, he gently pulled the horse back to the stall.

The Name of the Child

Leaning on the bedpost next to the window, Servet watched the snowfall in the early hours of twilight. She finally saw Avni walking toward the house with slow and measured steps. Smiling, she mused. *He is a very proud and handsome man. My mother must have been taken by his good looks and charmed by his sweet talk.*

It had been more than two years since she had married this young Ottoman officer. She had been barely fifteen years old when her mother had told her she would soon be wed. Servet still remembered the chills of fear and confusion that had overcome her at such a prospect. Months after learning the news, an overwhelming curiosity about the ongoing marriage negotiations had begun to drive her crazy. She wanted to see the man with whom she would share her life.

One rainy spring afternoon, thanks to much conniving and behind-the-scenes planning by her aunt, Servet was able to secretly watch her future husband riding a horse in his full Ottoman uniform. He was a slender, muscular man with a handsome, pale face, dark shiny eyes, short black hair, and a trimmed mustache. He was proudly and confidently riding a beautiful black stallion. His right hand firmly held the reins and his left hand rested on his sword. How excited she had been to observe the man she would soon marry.

When Avni entered the house, he spotted Servet looking out the window on the opposite side of the room. He gently called to her, "Servet, are you homesick again?"

Turning around, she walked toward her husband with a gleaming smile on her face. "How did you guess?" she asked sweetly. Noticing that Avni looked tired and annoyed, she helped him take off his coat.

"Avni," she inquired, "could you please tell me what's going on?"

To avoid answering the question, Avni jokingly responded, "It's a military secret."

Servet was not in the mood to be dismissed so casually. "Avni, let's be serious," she said. "I am worried. I'm afraid that something drastic may happen. I want us to be together. You have to talk to me now. Right now, right here."

Gently holding her arm, Avni asked her to move to the kitchen and sit down with him. As they faced each other across the kitchen table, Servet asked her husband if he was hungry.

"A cup of hot soup would be enough," Avni replied. After a short moment of silence, he continued, "Servet, I have to leave tomorrow for the front with a ragtag collection of recovered soldiers, untrained personnel, and local recruits. I have been ordered to lead these men to the northern Pristina front. This morning I had to give Mehmetali the terrible news of his younger son Huseyin's death. Poor Huseyin had been badly wounded and died before reaching Yanyevo. It was painful for me to tell his father the bad news. This afternoon Mehmetali helped me organize the group of conscripts from the villages, and he volunteered to join me on this dangerous mission. This crusty old Albanian is an amazing man!"

After a few spoonful of soup, Avni continued, "But there is good news. The colonel has decided that within a few days all the patients, personnel, and dependents in Yanyevo will be evacuated to Skopje. But I'm seriously worried about you and the baby. If you don't give birth to our child before the evacuation, it will be extremely uncomfortable and dangerous for you to travel. So, tell me how you feel. Do you think the baby is almost ready to be born?"

Laughing, Servet replied, "Avni, I wish it could happen tonight so that you would be around to see our newborn. Couldn't someone else take the men to the front? If you go to the front, I will worry so much about you. I'm scared to be alone with a newborn. You know, I'm almost ready to give birth to our first child. I should be happy and comfortable; instead, I feel scared and helpless."

Hoping to change the depressing mood into which they were both falling, Avni held his wife's hand. "What shall we name the child?" he asked.

Servet suggested that if it was a boy, Avni should choose the name. If it was a girl, she would choose.

Smiling broadly, Avni agreed, "I like the name 'Ilhami' for a boy."

Servet gladly approved Avni's suggestion. She liked the sound and meaning of the name. She looked adoringly at her husband. "If it's a girl," she murmured, "I'd like to name her Bedia."

New Year's Eve in Mitrovica

On the outskirts of Mitrovica, near the banks of the River Sitnica, which separates Kosovo from Serbia, a full moon vividly illuminated the conical shapes of the tents and rooftops of the officers' barracks of the Serbian nationalist army. The night was young, and the nationalist soldiers were getting ready to welcome the arrival of 1910.

Lieutenant Michailovitch, a lean and bony Serbian officer appearing intoxicated, left the staff mess hall in a hurry. He slammed the door behind him and walked straight into Burhan.

Detecting alcohol on Michailovitch's breath, Burhan moved away from the wobbly Serbian officer. Feeling nauseated, he decided against joining the crowd celebrating the Christian New Year. The smell of alcohol in the air reminded Burhan of a brutal incident that had recently occurred during the southern Serbian offensive.

While his military unit composed of irregular soldiers was following the retreating Ottoman ground forces, they had come across a small, defenseless Turkish village near Novi Bazaar in the Sanjak Province. The commander of the unit had suddenly and unexpectedly decided to attack the defenseless village. The merciless killings of local Turkish men and the rape of young women had compelled Burhan to renounce the savagery of war. Unfortunately, Burhan had not forgotten the similarly brutal event that had occurred in his hometown of Yanyevo a few years earlier. At that time, however, the cruel and ruthless treatment of people had left a different impact on his life: he had chosen to believe that violence begets violence. Now, after continuous exposure to the merciless destruction of lives and property, he rejected the supposed morality that prescribed an eye for an eye.

Sitting against the brick wall outside the mess hall, Burhan yearned for the usual stillness of the late evening hours. The loud noises from the ongoing celebration ensured that it was not going to be a quiet night. Feeling the strong cold wind blowing from the north, he muttered, "More snow on its way."

He realized that by focusing on the immediate natural surroundings he was trying to repress the horrific incident that had occurred in the Turkish village. He could still hear the young Turkish girl's screams for mercy as she was raped by four drunken soldiers in his company. He wished he had done something to stop it, but he had been afraid that such interference would reveal his Albanian identity.

When he had joined an irregular unit in the Serbian nationalist army, he had declared himself a Montenegrin Slavic Muslim and told the recruitment officer that he did not like Turks. However, he had not told the officer that his hatred of Turks stemmed from a vicious and brutal event that had happened in his hometown of Yanyevo. A couple of renegade Ottoman soldiers, who had escaped from an earlier confrontation in southern Serbia, had raped and killed several Serbian and Croatian women, including Burhan's childhood friend Katya.

Looking up to the sky and trying to hold back the flood of tears, he whispered, "Oh God, I miss her so much."

The First of January: Mehmetali to the Front

After completing his morning prayers, Mehmetali, a lean muscular man in his early-forties, walked toward the back-door of the coffeehouse. Stepping into snowy outdoors and feeling cold morning air seep into his bones, he regretted that he had to go outside to gather firewood. When he returned to the coffeehouse with an armload of wood, Jemal was in the kitchen waiting for him. Together they made a fire and prepared a pot of tea for Lieutenant Avni. Before leaving for the stable to get the lieutenant's horse ready for travel, Jemal asked Mehmetali to keep an eye on Lieutenant Avni during the journey to the front.

Mehmetali was impressed with Jemal's sincere concern for the lieutenant. "Jemal," he said. "I also have great respect for Lieutenant Avni. God willing, he will return safely from this trip and will meet his newborn child."

After Jemal had walked out of the kitchen, Mehmetali suddenly felt extremely tired. He had not been able to sleep much the night before; the death of his younger son and the unknown fate of Burhan, his older son, distressed him greatly. With great hope that he would find Burhan at the front, he volunteered to join Lieutenant Avni's troops. Mehmetali was not sure what he would tell his son if he ever saw him again. He just wanted to hug him, and perhaps convince him to return home.

Feeling disheartened and with tears rolling down his wrinkled cheeks, Mehmetali murmured, "The young ones are dying for old fools who are trying to save decaying empires ... and for what?"

Lieutenant Avni's Departure for the Front

The muezzin's call to morning prayer awakened Avni. He lit the candle next to the bed and watched Servet taking deep breaths in her sleep. He quietly left the bedroom and went into the kitchen. After performing ablutions with the cold water that was stored in the sink, he completed his morning prayers. Motionless and silent on his Anatolian prayer rug, he wondered about the dangers he might encounter during the next few days. Remembering his trip to Novi Bazaar, he prayed, "Oh great Lord, let me survive to see my family again."

He went back to the bedroom, lay down next to Servet, and felt her overgrown abdomen touch his hip. Her long beautiful arms slowly reached around his broad shoulders and pulled him gently to her. She whispered into his ear how handsome he was. Avni turned around and put both of his hands tenderly on Servet's abdomen.

"You have the beauty of an angel and the touch of a nymph."

Smiling, Servet agreed. "A very pregnant nymph indeed!"

A cold morning breeze brushed his face as Avni turned toward the house to glance at Servet one last time. Standing at the doorstep and looking utterly serene, she waved her hands and called out, "I'll be waiting for you in Skopje!"

As he took the reins of Yagiz from Jemal, Avni firmly said, "I'm counting on you to protect my family. As soon as my wife is ready to give birth, inform Doctor Nuri and Colonel Husnu. May the Lord protect us all."

"Yes, sir," Jemal replied stoutly. "I will make sure that your family gets to Skopje safely. May God give you strength and protect you."

Avni was now ready to lead a convoy of soldiers and supplies to Pristina. He gently pushed the heels of his riding boots into the horse's sides and pulled the reins to turn Yagiz around to go down the hill. Just before rounding the curve of the hillside to join the road to Pristina, Avni stopped abruptly and turned his horse around to have one final look at Yanyevo as he let the convoy pass him by. The natural beauty of the town as it appeared from that height and distance was impressive. Yanyevo was located in a valley squeezed between high rolling hills full of evergreens and deciduous trees. The wonderful combination of green trees, white patches of snow, and red roof tiles presented an overwhelmingly charming view.

Avni turned his horse around and disappointedly focused his eyes on the closer view in front of him: a long convoy of soldiers, some mounted on horses and some on foot, and numerous supply wagons and artillery pieces pulled by mules. Depressed by this overwhelming sight, he murmured, "This is a death march!"

The Third of January: The Pristina Front

Two days later, on the northern outskirts of Pristina, the ragtag Yanyevo troops joined the Ottoman defense lines. Mehmetali, serving Avni his usual large cup of morning tea, noticed that the lieutenant looked ill at ease. Avni saw the inquisitive look on Mehmetali's face. Without being asked, he told his trusted old friend the disturbing news he had received early that morning.

"Instructions from the command center for our unit have arrived," he said remorsefully. "Within a few days, we are to join the southeastern flank of the defense lines. Together with the Albanian irregulars, a major Serbian army thrust toward Pristina is expected to stem from a location somewhere over the hills -- east of Mitrovica. If we fail to stop this frontal attack, both Pristina and Yanyevo will be threatened by the enemy. I want you to select a reliable soldier you know and trust. Send him to Yanyevo to deliver this envelope to Colonel Husnu. I pray that Lieutenant Nihad has prepared a proper defense strategy for the evacuation. I sincerely hope that he has been informed that the Serbian army and Albanian nationalist irregulars might soon be blocking the road to Skopje."

Mehmetali hurriedly responded, "Lieutenant, I will immediately send one of the local recruits back to Yanyevo with your letter to the colonel. But sir, with your permission, I would like to ask a question: since we are going into battle in a few days, will we be able to stop the advance of the enemy forces?"

"I wish I knew the answer, my friend, but I don't. We just have to put up a good fight. The rest is beyond our control."

Mehmetali walked out into the cold air and started to stroll through hundreds of tents. The campground, though full of soldiers, looked strangely desolate. Enduring the gusty, cold winter winds in their makeshift tents, the soldiers, exhausted from many days of travel, seemed drained of energy, as forlorn as wandering ghosts.

Upon reaching the tents of the Yanyevo troops, Mehmetali summoned the youngest recruit and ordered him to deliver the lieutenant's note to Colonel Husnu in Yanyevo. He told the young messenger not to return to Pristina. "Instead, you will report to Lieutenant Nihad."

After the messenger's departure, Mehmetali carefully thought about how he would find his older son Burhan. Just a few weeks earlier, he had received a message from a wounded soldier that Burhan had been sighted with the Serbian nationalist forces during the Sanjak Province defense operations. If the news were true and Burhan was still alive, he would now be on the other side of the border. Mehmetali could not stop thinking about the possibility of seeing Burhan again. *If they win the battle and we both stay alive,* he mused, *I may see him again. Maybe we will win the coming battle and Burhan will become our prisoner.* "Wishful thinking!" he mumbled.

He knew well that both the Ottomans and the Serbs quickly executed prisoners. His overwhelming desire to see his older son again seemed hopeless. He wondered. *Why am I here? Everything and everyone in my life has disappeared. Burhan is my last connection to life.* He took his prayer beads out of his pocket and started to pray. "My Lord," he whispered. "Even if I have to die soon, let me see my son once more and hold his face in my hands."

Burhan's Secret Mission

Meanwhile, at the Serbian nationalist camp in Mitrovica, Burhan had been ordered to report immediately to Commander Karaevitch. Entering the smoke-filled central command room, Karaevitch's assistant ordered Burhan to sit and wait until everyone but the commander had departed.

After everyone was gone, Commander Karaevitch lit a cigarette and ordered Burhan to approach. Walking around the massive table full of maps, Burhan, a twenty-two-year-old, tall and well-built Kosovo Albanian, moved toward the middle-aged, short and stout Serbian commander. Leaning on the table, Karaevitch swiftly pulled a revolver from the drawer and placed it on a map spread over the table. Burhan suddenly felt threatened. He wondered if his true identity had been discovered. But then, he rationalized, he would not have been allowed to enter this room if the commander knew his true identity.

"Son," said the commander. "You've been recommended by Lieutenant Michailovitch to conduct a special mission for our regiment. I understand you're a Montenegrin Muslim. I presume you speak Turkish as well as Albanian?"

"Yes, sir, I'm fluent in both languages."

Karaevitch continued his inquiry. "I want you to be aware that this is a very dangerous mission. You are expected to infiltrate the Ottoman lines to determine the overall military strength of the enemy and identify infantry and artillery positions."

The commander pointed at the tip of the gun that he had placed on the map and asked Burhan to move closer to the table. "This location is Kosovo Polje," he said. "It is also called the Field of Blackbirds. We suspect that the Ottomans may launch a counter-attack from this location during our coming offensive."

Burhan remembered that the Field of Blackbirds was the famous Kosovo battleground where, more than five hundred years earlier, the Ottoman Turks had destroyed the Serbian army led by Tsar Lazar.

As he leaned over the table to find the location of the historic battleground on the map, Burhan said, "Sir, this duty would be a great honor for me. We don't want history to repeat itself."

Karaevitch nodded approvingly. "Tomorrow morning," he said, "you'll be wearing a proper Ottoman uniform. You'll receive detailed instructions on how to conduct an intelligence mission. Now, hand me your revolver."

Burhan nervously gave his gun to Commander Karaevitch.

After placing Burhan's gun in the drawer, Karaevitch picked up the revolver on the map. Handing it to Burhan, he said, "This is an authentic Ottoman revolver. You must wear this gun during your mission behind Ottoman lines. I look forward to your safe return within seventy-two hours."

The Fourth of January: Finding the Collaborator

The next morning, Burhan received his instructions, along with the Ottoman uniform of a military police sergeant. After he put on his new outfit, he was taken through the woods on horseback to the outskirts of a village near the Ottoman front. Before departing for the village, he was told to contact the head of the village, a Kosovo Albanian named Ismet. Burhan would receive logistical support as well as military information from this man, who was known to be a reliable informer and collaborator. Burhan then was instructed to return to the same location in the woods in exactly seventy-two hours for the return trip to Mitrovica.

As he walked through the woods, Burhan thought about the dangers that would threaten his life during the next three days. What if he ran into someone from his village? That would be the end of him; he would be summarily executed. He pushed the thought out of his mind; he could not imagine anyone from Yanyevo being around Pristina. He also felt that because his appearance had changed considerably since his departure from Yanyevo, no one would recognize him. He now had very short hair and a full mustache. He firmly believed that as long as he kept a safe distance from the Ottoman troops, he would be fine. He had no desire to be close enough to anyone who might recognize him. His mission required only observation from afar in order to determine troop concentrations and artillery positions. Burhan hoped that these distant observations would enable him to make an educated guess about the location of the anticipated enemy counterattack.

When he entered the village, Burhan was extremely careful. He skirted the edge of the forest to find a safe entry point into the populated area. He discreetly found his way into one of the side streets near the forest. To avoid suspicion, he walked confidently toward the village center. He then casually stopped in front of an older gentleman who was sitting on the stairs to his house and sipping his morning tea.

"Uncle," Burhan asked, "where is the village headman's house?" Burhan made this inquiry to find out Ismet's whereabouts as well as to legitimize his presence in the village.

The old man, raising his thick eyebrows, examined the young Ottoman soldier. "My dear sergeant," he said solemnly. "The head of the village was arrested by the local police a few days ago. Now why are you, a military policeman, looking for him?" Without waiting for an answer, the old man continued, "Go down to the end of the road and turn left. You'll see the coffeehouse on your right. Inside you'll find the village headman being questioned by the local police chief. Tell me now, what has Ismet done?"

Burhan, feeling awkward and nervous, sternly answered the old man's question, "Uncle, I cannot talk about it. I thank you for the directions to the coffeehouse."

He immediately walked away from the old man to avoid further questions, thinking that wearing an Ottoman military police uniform had been a very good idea indeed. As he walked down the road toward the village center, Burhan decided to visit the coffeehouse to observe the ongoing interrogation of the village headman and gather information that might prove useful for his mission. He cautiously entered the smoke-filled room. Even though it was crowded, the place was strangely quiet. In the far right corner of the large room, he saw several policemen sitting around a middle-aged man. Burhan decided to be close to where the action was and slowly moved toward a table near the inquisition. He was abruptly stopped by an annoyingly aggressive policeman.

As he held Burhan's arm, the policeman gruffly said, "Sergeant, it took you a long time to get here!" He then asked Burhan to sit next to him at the table where the village headman was being questioned. Staring sternly at Burhan, he continued, "We've received several reports that the head of this village is an informer for the Serbian nationalists. We have strict orders to arrest all informers and collaborators. We are to execute them if there is sufficient evidence. If the evidence is not sufficient, we keep them in jail until more proof is found. In this man's case, he is without doubt an informer and a collaborator. He was caught leaving written messages to his nationalist contact at an established pickup point. He was supposed to be executed today. But a few days ago, I received a message from the military intelligence unit that the prisoner is to be taken to the Pristina Military Headquarters for further questioning. He is all yours, Sergeant. Would you mind if I attach a policeman to accompany you to the headquarters?"

"There is no need for that," replied Burhan. "I'll take him to headquarters myself. You need your men here to catch more people like him. May I have something to eat before taking him to Pristina? I haven't had anything this morning."

As he was about to finish eating his hearty breakfast, the prisoner was brought before him. The village headman's hands were tied behind his back. He appeared to be around fifty years of age, in good physical condition, and garbed in expensive clothes. He seemed to be a wealthy man.

Burhan roughly guided the prisoner out of the coffeehouse and commenced their long walk toward Pristina. He estimated that the journey would take slightly more than four hours if they took the main road a few kilometers behind the front lines. Burhan felt extremely lucky. *I could use this man as cover while I walk through the front lines,* he thought. *I could pretend that I had just taken charge of the prisoner in the last village. Together with him, I could continue with my secret mission all the way through the front lines.*

Burhan, aware of the fact that he had been handed a man full of information, decided to get everything he could out of Ismet. "You are a dead man, Ismet," Burhan said. "And you know it. Why did you do this? Why did you take the side of the enemy?"

In a very confident tone of voice, Ismet replied, "Sergeant, I'm a rational man. I'm a landowner. We both know who will win the coming battles. The Ottoman army has no chance of winning this conflict. By helping the nationalists, I wanted to secure the safety of my family and my village."

Burhan responded, "Do you think a new master would be any better than the old one?"

"I don't know about that, Sergeant," replied Ismet. "But what I do know is that a new master is on his way to take over our lands. For us Albanians, a very precarious future is in the making. Maybe this conflict will offer us a chance to establish a country of our own."

Burhan remembered how often he had had similar thoughts about the future of the Albanians. While most Albanians had chosen to remain on the side of the Ottoman state, some under the leadership of Isa Boletin, the former head of the Ottoman Sultan's personal Albanian palace guards, had seriously questioned the unstable status of the Albanians residing in southern Serbia and Kosovo. This area of conflict was home to a mixture of Albanian, Serbian, Croat, and Turkish villages.

In one quick move, Burhan pushed Ismet off the main road and into a thinly wooded area. He ordered him to sit down. As he knelt down next to his prisoner, Burhan contemplated various strategies for maximizing his access to the information in Ismet's mind.

After a long, silent moment, Burhan said, "I'm an Albanian, and I agree with most of what you've just said. I've been fighting the Ottomans on the side of the Serbian nationalist forces for a year. I'm now on a special mission to collect information on troop movements and artillery locations. I was asked by the nationalist command unit to find you and seek your help in gathering information. You're lucky that I came into the coffeehouse this morning. Now, you must tell me everything you know about the Ottoman defense preparations. I'll take the information back to nationalist headquarters. You can also help me identify strategic troop movements and artillery locations while we both move around the front lines. We'll continue to pretend that you're a prisoner and that I'm the military police sergeant taking you to headquarters for interrogation."

As Ismet listened intently to Burhan, he thought, *This is too much of a coincidence to believe! This sergeant wants me to voluntarily disclose the information I sent to the nationalists over the last two months so that the Ottomans can formulate proper military countermeasures. How smart! Maybe I will pretend that I believe him, and give him false information on the existing military logistics. That would be an added victory for me before I'm executed.*

He turned toward Burhan. "Look, Sergeant," he said. "I don't have much choice but to believe that you're telling the truth. If I'm wrong, it does not matter; I'm a dead man anyway. But, if you're telling the truth, both of us will survive and make a final assessment of the military situation. What exactly do you want me to do, Sergeant?"

Burhan stood up and spoke calmly. "As we walk, you should tell me what you think the Ottomans are up to. How are they planning to defend southern Kosovo? We heard about a plan for a counterattack. Where do you think it will take place?"

During the next hour or so, as they walked, Burhan and Ismet talked and watched the military panorama from a safe distance. They could see troop movements and artillery concentrations on the horizon. They passed many infantry units and artillery pieces. From these observations it was impossible to guess where exactly the Ottoman counteroffensive might begin. Burhan noticed that the defense lines were well supported by troops and artillery. In addition to infantry, he noticed a strong presence of cavalry. The Ottoman defense lines appeared much stronger than what the nationalists had assumed.

He told Ismet that the coming battle would be a very bloody one. He strongly emphasized that the Ottoman defensive positions appeared solid and would not be easily broken. As he spoke, Burhan clearly realized the nationalists' concerns about the possibility of an Ottoman counter-attack. Apparently, the Ottoman army had established this colossal military force to seize their chance to push the Serbian nationalists back to southern Serbia. As he continued to observe the Ottoman defensive preparations, Burhan seriously wondered if a military reversal was indeed possible. He concluded that it was not probable, given that a substantial quantity of military hardware and thousands of well-trained volunteers had recently arrived from the Austro-Hungarian Empire to support the Serbian nationalists' cause. When he compared it to what he had seen in the field, Burhan became confused about the information he had received from Ismet. His prisoner had mentioned that the counter-attack was expected to come from the northeastern section of the Pristina defense lines, not from the southwestern part as had been reported during his meeting with Commander Karaevitch in Mitrovica. Burhan wondered if the commander was the one who had received wrong information from an unreliable source. He had no reason to doubt Ismet's information. Since he had saved Ismet's life, Burhan did not expect to be misled by his prisoner.

While staying in close proximity to Pristina, Burhan and Ismet moved cautiously in and out along the defensive lines. On several occasions, they were questioned by military rear-defense guards. Burhan's story and the presence of the prisoner helped prevent any serious problems. Toward the end of the day, they moved away from the lines, hoping to find shelter so they could spend the night in relative safety. Before nightfall, they finally found an abandoned barn. Fortunately, during their long walk they had acquired some basic rations.

After they had finished their trifling meal in the dark, smelly barn, Burhan asked Ismet to hold his hands together in front of his chest. "Sorry, brother!" he said, "I must tie your hands in case soldiers surprise us during the night. Tomorrow morning, we'll continue our trip toward the defense lines east of Pristina."

Ismet, realizing that his opportunity to escape during the night had vanished, silently cursed his bad luck. With his tied hands, he struggled for a long time to pull the blanket over his head.

The Fifth of January: Behind the Ottoman Lines

The next morning, Burhan awoke to the noise of galloping horses. Peering through the cracks in the barn door, he saw a large Ottoman cavalry regiment moving swiftly southwest, probably toward Kosovo Polje, the Field of Blackbirds. He noticed many artillery pieces among the supplies wagons in this sudden logistical relocation. He shook Ismet to wake him up. Once the long column of cavalry and artillery pieces had disappeared into the distance, Burhan and his prisoner resumed their walk behind the front lines. Burhan now felt that Karaevitch's prediction of the Ottoman counterattack positions had been valid. The size and the direction of the cavalry relocation in the very early hours of the morning had indicated the possible site of the counterattack.

Realizing that Ismet had been lying all along, Burhan mused, *I should get rid of the bastard as soon as I confirm the exact locations of troop concentrations for the counterattack.* He knew that he had only forty-eight hours left to complete his mission and return to the outskirts of the village where the nationalist soldiers had left him. Noticing that his prisoner was dragging his feet, Burhan ordered Ismet to walk faster.

As soon as they entered the newly formed defensive lines, they were stopped by a group of infantry rear-guards. Burhan was quick in responding to the questions of the infantry sergeant major. While he explained that he was escorting a prisoner to the command center in northeastern Pristina, he took out the papers that the village police chief had given him. Unfortunately, the papers clearly indicated that the prisoner was to be taken to the military intelligence unit at Pristina headquarters. As he handed over the papers, Burhan hoped that the sergeant major would not pay attention to the details.

The sergeant major quickly glanced at Burhan's papers. "You have a long journey ahead of you," he said. "I hope you're aware of the fact that the command center has recently moved to a new location east of the old cemetery." Returning the papers to Burhan without reading the details, he wished Burhan a safe journey.

As the infantry company disappeared into the defensive lines, Burhan turned to Ismet.

"Luck was on our side this time!"

In response, Ismet mumbled, "My dear Sergeant, I'm starving. We should have asked them to give us some food."

Also feeling hunger pains in his gut, Burhan agreed. "I am hungry as well. However, it is not going to be easy to find a place to eat. We are far from any settlement where we might find food. Our only chance is to get some from an infantry service unit on our way. We'll continue our journey until we reach the newly relocated strategic command center. Then we'll return to your village."

Ismet reacted immediately. "Sergeant," he said loudly. "What exactly are you planning to do with me when we get back to my village?"

Burhan suppressed his true feeling that he should put a bullet into Ismet's head for having lied to him. "I'll set you free," he replied. "You have to take care of yourself."

Ismet, grunting to indicate his agreement, thought that what Burhan had suggested was too good to believe. He did not trust Burhan and could not figure out what he was trying to do; he still thought Burhan was an Ottoman intelligence officer pretending to be a Serbian nationalist infiltrator.

Father Meets Son

Lieutenant Avni ordered Mehmetali to lead a few men to the armory and bring in the ammunition allocated to the Yanyevo unit. Mehmetali asked the lieutenant's permission to use his horse, Yagiz, to pull the ammunition cart which was usually pulled by soldiers. Grinning, Avni nodded. "See if you can get something good to eat as you pass the provisions unit. I hear it is controlled by local Albanians," he said to Mehmetali who was about to depart.

Mehmetali, stifling his laughter, replied, "How about if I get us some Albanian-style fried liver and pilaf?"

Knowing that Lieutenant Avni would not mind, Mehmetali rode the horse to the armory. The four soldiers who would help Mehmetali load the ammunition at the armory followed him on foot. On the way, Mehmetali noticed a civilian being roughed around in a large crowd of soldiers. The civilian was accompanied by a military policeman. Pulling the reins to stop the horse, he wondered why a civilian was among the soldiers. When the military policeman who was leading the civilian through the crowd got closer to him, Mehmetali realized that the soldier looked exactly like his son Burhan. As he moved the horse toward the civilian and the military policeman, Mehmetali kept repeating, "It is not possible! It is not possible! It cannot be him!"

Burhan, pulling Ismet along, began whispering, "We'd better move faster and change direction. I saw a couple of military guards looking at us. Let's quickly move behind those tents on the right." They rushed toward the cluster of infantry tents.

Mehmetali, noticing that the civilian and the soldier had disappeared behind the tents, dismounted and asked one of the soldiers to hold the horse. He then ran toward the tents where he had last seen them disappear. As Mehmetali ran around the corner of a dense cluster of tents, he came face-to-face with his son.

"Burhan, my son, what are you doing here?"

Recognizing his father, Burhan put his hand over Mehmetali's mouth. "Say no more! Father, say no more!"

They embraced for a long moment. Mehmetali asked Burhan to stay where he was, and ran back to tell his men to move the horse and the cart to the armory to load the ammunition. He said he would catch up with them later. He returned to where he had left Burhan and sat down with him on the ground between some tents.

Burhan was saddened by the unfortunate news of his younger brother's fate. After a short moment of silence, he explained to his father why he was behind the Ottoman defensive lines.

Mehmetali responded, "Son, I should shoot you right now!" He reached out and held Burhan's shoulder. "Why you're here doesn't matter to me. I'm glad to see you!"

Burhan asked his father about the location of the Yanyevo troops. As his father told him where they were located, he marked the location on his map.

"Father, I'll give you information that might save your life and the lives of others, too. If you are able to pass this information on to the Ottoman authorities, you might save their lives as well. The nationalist army recently received a new supply of weapons, including heavy artillery equipment from various European countries. In addition to that, a very large group of infantry volunteers from the Austro-Hungarian Empire has joined the nationalist army in the last few weeks. It seems that most of these volunteers are well-trained regular infantry conscripts from the Austro-Hungarian army. I have seen most of the Ottoman defensive preparations. Though they look impressive, I don't think the Ottomans have any chance of winning this coming battle."

Mehmetali was greatly disturbed by this information. He told his son that he would not be able to pass this information to anyone. "First of all," Mehmetali said, "no one would believe me. Secondly, I would be punished for spreading lies about the strength of the enemy."

Understanding the situation, Burhan changed the subject and told his father about Ismet and his ordeal. He then asked his father where they might find some food. Mehmetali told Burhan to wait for him. He ran to the nearest supplies unit to get some food and water for them.

After Mehmetali's departure Ismet commented, "Your father is on the side of the Ottomans and you claim to be on the side of the Serbian nationalists?"

"Of course," said Burhan. "That is exactly how it is. Isn't this true for many Albanian families?"

"You're right, Burhan. My older brother remains an officer in the Ottoman army and my younger brother recently joined the Albanian insurgents led by Idris Seferi. They are organizing themselves to fight against the Ottoman army in southwestern Kosovo. And I am, strange as it may seem, on the side of the Serbians. I have already told you why I've decided to help the Serbian nationalists: a mere survival tactic. Tell me, why did you decide to help the nationalist cause?"

"It's a long, sad story. Maybe I'll tell you later."

A short while later, Mehmetali returned with some packaged food and two canteens of water. As he took the packages from his father, Burhan said, "It's time for us to move on."

It was very hard for both of them to say farewell.

"You know, my son," Mehmetali said. "Two days ago, I prayed that I might hold your face in my hands before I die. Here we are!"

He slowly raised his arms toward the handsome face of his son and put his large hands around it.

"May the good Lord protect you, my son."

"We both need His protection, Father," Burhan replied. "I pray that we'll soon see each other again."

As he waved farewell to his father, Burhan told Ismet that their reconnaissance mission must be completed before sunset at the latest. At dusk, they would have to return to the barn where they had spent the previous night.

Hours later, when they sat down in the vacant barn to eat what Mehmetali had given them, Ismet reached out and touched Burhan's shoulder with tightly roped hands. In a voice trembling with sincerity, he said, "My brother, please forgive me for not believing you and for telling you lies about the Ottoman troop movements. Take out your map; I'll show you what is really going to happen."

Burhan slowly took the map out of his pocket and put it on the ground. He then reached toward Ismet and untied his hands.

The Sixth of January: Young Turks in Charge

Before entering Lieutenant Commander Mahmud's tent, Avni straightened his uniform and removed his fez, placing it under his left arm. This was the first time he was to meet the newly appointed commander of the third regiment of the Ottoman army, which was defending the northeastern flank of the front. After formal introductions, the commander gave a long-winded speech repeatedly mentioning how close he was to Shevket Turgut Pasha, the commander general of the Ottoman forces in Kosovo. Avni felt that his new commanding officer, lacking previous battle experience, appeared overly self-confident and arrogant. Earlier in the day, he had heard from other junior officers that the commander had risen quickly in the ranks because of his family's connection to a powerful concubine in the sultan's harem.

In order to enable the senior staff to work on the defensive strategy with the new commander, junior officers were asked to leave the command center and return to their respective units. As they left the command center, Avni tried to reassure his colleagues that the battle-hardened senior staff would compensate for the new commander's noticeable lack of leadership.

Avni followed the other junior officers to the mess tent for morning tea and conversation about the vicious political games that were being played at the Ottoman capital. Since the overthrow of Sultan Abdul Hamid by the Young Turk movement a year earlier, the Ottoman government had suffered a series of political crises, one after another. These political setbacks had resulted in several drastic military defeats, particularly in southern Europe. A new Ottoman government had recently been formed under the leadership of Enver Pasha. Most of the junior officers in the mess tent were celebrating the renewed political strength of the Young Turks.

His mind preoccupied by his wife's predicament, Avni could not get involved in the heated political discussions. He dwelt on the responsibilities of becoming a father, and was worried about his wife's health and security. Before the conversation ended, Avni left the mess tent and returned to the Yanyevo detachment with the hope of a message from Colonel Husnu informing him of his child's birth.

Avni found Mehmetali sitting with a group of Yanyevo soldiers. He asked if there was any news from Yanyevo.

"I've not received anything yet, Lieutenant."

Avni ordered Mehmetali to gather all the troop leaders for a briefing on defense responsibilities. A few minutes later, facing the eight troop leaders, Avni told them that they would move to the northeastern periphery of the Field of Blackbirds the following day. He explained that they would be expected to provide backup to the main infantry regiment, which would also be supported by the cavalry and the heavy artillery units positioned in the northeastern hills.

After attending to the details of the next day's planned relocation, Avni sat in front of his tent. As he watched the snow beginning to fall, he sipped a cup of Turkish coffee prepared by

Mehmetali. The landscape under the bright blue western sky was breathtaking. Gazing at the dark clouds gradually blocking the noon sun, he thought constantly of Servet. He wondered if she had received his letter, which had been sent along with his message to Colonel Husnu.

A Turkish Village in Despair

Burhan and Ismet were already on their way back to Ismet's village when they had to change direction due to frequent encounters with the infantry military guards. They turned south to skirt the busy main road. As they walked through the uncultivated fields, they were suddenly and unexpectedly surrounded by several armed men.

Pointing his gun directly at Burhan, the leader of the band asked in Turkish who they were. He was a very tall and bulky man who appeared old but strong. Burhan was confused; since he was in an Ottoman soldier's uniform, why had the old Turkish man asked him to identify himself? Burhan sensed that their lives now depended on what he told this threatening man.

When Burhan slowly reached into his jacket pocket, the old man told him to stop. He walked toward Burhan, reached into his pocket, and took out the papers. Without looking at him, the old man asked the others to search the prisoners carefully.

While he was searched, Burhan studied the burly old man. He noticed that the old man was holding the papers upside down; obviously he was illiterate. Burhan was still not sure whose life was being threatened: his or Ismet's. If these rough and agitated Turkish men discovered that Ismet was an informer, they would shoot him on the spot. Since they had shown no respect for his Ottoman uniform, he reasoned that they would probably kill him as well and then bury them to conceal the evidence. He realized that he now had to think fast in order to save their lives.

Burhan quickly figured out why these old Turkish men were so agitated and aggressive. They were probably a group of villagers moving with their families to safer ground in case the Ottomans should lose the coming battle. Hoping that his reasoning was correct, he talked to the burly old man in Turkish.

"Father, my name is Burhan. I'm a security guard attached to Ismet Bey, who is the special representative of the Ottoman governor in Skopje." As he waited for the man's response, Burhan looked at Ismet, hoping that he had the capacity to understand the seriousness of the situation.

The old man loudly asked Burhan, "Where are you going?"

"We are on our way to deliver the written instructions you have in your hands to all Ottoman army commanders in the field. This direct order from Istanbul instructs the army to evacuate the Turkish villages located near the defense lines to safer areas."

The old man handed the papers back to Burhan, asking forgiveness for his crude behavior. He then ordered his men to lower their guns and asked Burhan and Ismet to follow him.

After half an hour of walking through a patch of forested land, they reached a large Turkish village. In the main square of the village, Burhan saw confirmation of his guess that the entire village was ready to move somewhere safer. There were ox carts and mule buggies full of belongings, and domesticated animals of every kind tied to long leads. There were women, young and old, surrounded by many children.

Settling under a canvas shelter, the old village head told Burhan and Ismet that his name is Selim and asked them to sit and eat some bread and barley soup with him. While they were eating, Selim, the village head, solemnly explained the villagers' fears. "Everyone in my village knows what happened to the Turkish villages in Sanjak

Province in southern Serbia after the nationalists won and took over those areas. More than a month ago, the Ottoman military sent official messages to all Turkish and Muslim villages in Kosovo that no one would be permitted to relocate."

Selim, raising his voice, continued his complaint against this unreasonable decision by the military authorities. "This has been our village for centuries," he growled. "Over the hill to the south of us there is a Croat village. A few kilometers east of the Croat village there is an Albanian village, and little more than ten kilometers north of us lays a Serbian village. Over the centuries, all these villages coexisted peacefully. Now, we, the Turks, have become the enemy in our own country. If the Ottoman army thinks we're running away to save our skins, they're damn right. What else can we do? Stay here and wait to be slaughtered? That's not a smart thing to do. The enemy has no mercy!"

After a long pause, the village head continued, "In the Sanjak Province, many Turkish, Albanian, and Slavic Muslim families were completely wiped out. The same will happen here. We have to move to safer ground. If the Ottoman army wins the next battle, we will return to our village. If not, we'll start a new life in a land where there is peace and security."

Burhan completely understood what Selim meant. During the southern Serbia campaigns by the nationalist army, he had seen plenty of vicious attacks on Muslim villages. These villages had been completely destroyed, and most of the inhabitants had been killed.

Ismet, finally comprehending the importance of the issues that were being discussed, interrupted. He promised Selim that he would discuss with the Ottoman army authorities all the matters that had been brought to his attention. He then quickly thanked Selim for the meal and asked permission to depart so he could perform his duty and inform the military authorities that they should allow the

Turkish villagers to move into safer areas in southeast Kosovo, or possibly into some agricultural settlements in Macedonia.

Burhan, knowing the dangers facing these villagers, interrupted. "Selim Efendi," he said politely. "Since you're already prepared for the journey, why don't you start moving toward southern Kosovo as soon as possible?"

Selim rose to his feet to see them off. "Son," he said deliberately, "we've already decided to do that. We thought you were coming here to order us not to move. We were going to shoot both of you. I'm glad we decided to ask questions first."

Later, as they walked toward the main road, Burhan and Ismet congratulated each other on being clever and staying alive.

Painful Memories

Burhan and Ismet reached Ismet's village just before sunset. Ismet suggested they wait until dark before entering the village. Understanding Ismet's fear of being recognized, Burhan agreed. They settled in a wooded area secluded from the main road to the village and waited for darkness. Ismet asked Burhan why he disliked Turks so much.

Burhan stared off into space for a long time before answering. "I don't hate the Turks," he replied. "Not anymore. I realized that when we were with the old men of the Turkish village this morning. I just don't like what the Ottomans have done in the Balkans for the last decade. There has been so much destruction and death! I grew up in Yanyevo. In my town, the Turks, Croats, Serbs, and Albanians have lived together for centuries. As children, we all played together in the streets, and we were all good friends. Katya, a Croat girl, was my very special friend. We were in love. We were planning to escape to Vienna at the first opportunity to start a life together. I don't know if we really could have done that. Maybe it was just a dream, but it was truly a beautiful dream. I would have done anything to have a life together with her."

With emotional strain on his face, Burhan continued with his story. "Two years ago, our dream became a nightmare. One dreadful day, she was raped and killed by a group of Ottoman irregular soldiers who had been booted out of southern Serbia by the nationalists. They were looking for someone helpless on whom to take their revenge. Katya was in the wrong place at the wrong time. Because of that incident, last year I joined the Serbian nationalist forces to fight against the cruel Ottoman rule. Now I've got to admit that the nationalists are equally cruel. Obviously, in any war there will be conflicts that result in death and destruction. I don't understand why there is so much unnecessary violence against innocent people and harmless bystanders. Why are so many innocent children killed, so many young women raped, and so many villages completely destroyed? These are all wrong and immoral activities. To me, a proper path to independence should never include cruelty and unnecessary violence."

Ismet was moved by Burhan's tragic story. He reminded Burhan that he was a handsome young man and had a long life ahead of him. "You know, Burhan," Ismet said, "one day, when you least expect it, you'll fall in love again."

Burhan sullenly responded, "That might be true, but only if I survive the battles we face over the next few days."

Back to Ismet's Village

In the evening hours just after sunset, Burhan and Ismet cautiously entered the village. Ismet suggested that they stay at his house for the night. Early the following morning, they would be able to go to the forest to meet the group of nationalist soldiers waiting for Burhan. As they walked along the winding, narrow streets of the village, Burhan was reminded of his arrival at this Turkish-Albanian village barely three days before.

Ismet stopped in front of his house and softly knocked on the door. A man's voice asked, in Albanian, for the identity of the person knocking on the door. After Ismet identified himself, the door was opened. He immediately told the man who had opened the door to keep quiet; he did not want a commotion that might be noticed by the neighbors. He told the man to take the children and women away, except for his wife. They should not learn of his safe return home.

"If they know nothing, it is safer for them," Ismet reminded the man. "They will, without realizing it, protect me and my friend here. Uncle, let me introduce you to Burhan, a soldier in the Serbian nationalist army who, by mere luck, saved my life."

Ismet's uncle gave Burhan a warm welcome and asked them to come into the house. Ismet and Burhan then sat and waited while Ismet's uncle cleared the premises of women and children.

Leaning against the back of the old wooden chair, Ismet told Burhan that the man was his uncle from his mother's side. Then Ismet went on to explain that he had been supporting a large extended family, including the family of his older brother who was serving in the Ottoman army.

A few minutes later, Ismet's uncle returned and asked them to move into the main family room. "We all thought you were dead," he said. "Your wife is crying in the bedroom. She would like to see you immediately. She cannot believe you are home alive."

As he was leaving the room, Ismet asked Burhan to relax, make himself at home, and rest until a meal was prepared for them. Moments later, a young man with a lame leg came in with a cup of hot tea. Limping as he moved, he introduced himself as the eldest son of Ismet's brother. He asked Burhan how and why an Ottoman soldier had saved his uncle's life.

Burhan was exhausted and in no mood to talk. He firmly but gently suggested that the young man, whose name was Dursun, ask his uncle for the story. The young man tersely excused himself and left the room. Lying on a floor divan in the warm room, Burhan immediately fell asleep.

Half an hour later, Ismet touched Burhan's shoulder to wake him for the evening meal. Four men, including Ismet's uncle and nephew, sat on the wooden floor around a circular table full of freshly cooked Albanian dishes. While they ate, Ismet answered the questions of his two relatives. During the meal, Burhan learned that the day after he and Ismet had left the village, two military police sergeants had arrived to take Ismet to Pristina headquarters. They had been told by the local police chief that Ismet had been taken to the headquarters the day before by a military police sergeant. Because Ismet had disappeared into thin air, the military police took the chief of police with them to Pristina for questioning.

Ismet's uncle commented that most of the villagers thought the police chief would never be seen again. Ismet, with a happy grin on his face, responded to his uncle, "My return is the guarantee that the chief constable will never be back."

Since there was a chance that the military police would return to search for Ismet, Burhan suggested that they leave early in the morning. After discussing family matters for a few more minutes, Ismet's uncle and nephew excused themselves for the night and left the room. Handing a blanket to Burhan, Ismet told him that he would wake him up before the morning prayers.

Alone once again in the large family room, Burhan lay down on the divan. Feeling tired and well fed, he quickly fell asleep.

The Seventh of January: the Birth

Fatma Hanim, head nurse at the Yanyevo military hospital, tiptoed toward Jemal who was sound asleep on the kitchen floor by the stove. Gently touching his shoulder, she asked him to fetch Doctor Nuri immediately. Jumping quickly to his feet, Jemal looked at the clock on the wall; it was a few minutes after midnight. He left the house and ran toward Doctor Nuri's house without his overcoat. He painfully felt the damp, cold air penetrating all the way to his bones. Within a few minutes, he reached the doctor's house. Holding the lantern at face-level, Jemal identified himself and announced, "Servet Hanim is ready to give birth."

Jemal waited outside while Doctor Nuri got dressed. As they hurried toward Lieutenant Avni's house, the doctor told Jemal to inform Colonel Husnu. Jemal abruptly asked, "At this time of the night?" Doctor Nuri promptly replied, "Colonel Husnu asked me to inform him immediately when Servet Hanim was ready to give birth. So go wake him and tell him what is going on."

With a broad smile, Colonel Husnu welcomed Jemal's news about the upcoming birth. He ordered Jemal to find the soldier who had brought the message from Lieutenant Avni a few days earlier.

"Tell him to be ready for immediate travel to Pristina after the birth of the child. He should make sure that the good news is delivered to the lieutenant personally." Before closing the door, Colonel Husnu told Jemal that he would visit Servet Hanim in the morning.

Jemal ran to the soldiers' barracks. He was happy to get indoors to warm his freezing feet. He did not know the young soldier's name, so it took a long time to locate him in the infantry soldiers' sleeping quarters. The night guard told Jemal that the soldier he was seeking, named Avni, was asleep at the far left end of the sleeping quarters. Jemal woke the young soldier and told him to get ready to deliver a message to Lieutenant Avni in Pristina. As he gave instructions to the young soldier, Jemal removed his shoes and socks, placed his frozen feet next to the stove, and rubbed his toes.

Proud to have accomplished so much in the past hour, Jemal strolled back to Lieutenant Avni's house at a leisurely pace. As he entered the house, he came face-to-face with Doctor Nuri.

"Jemal," the doctor yelled excitedly. "The baby has been born. It's a girl." Hearing the news, Jemal turned around and walked out of the house. Doctor Nuri, standing at the door, shouted behind Jemal, "Where are you going?"

"I've got to inform Lieutenant Avni that he's a father now," replied Jemal.

Doctor Nuri smiled. "It's a long way to Pristina, son," he bellowed. "You should take a horse."

Turning around and walking backward toward the barracks, Jemal shouted back, "Thank you for the suggestion, Doctor, but I've received my instructions from the colonel. I must send the soldier Avni to the front to inform Lieutenant Avni." He then spun around and ran toward the soldiers' quarters.

Inside the house, Servet sat up in her bed and snuggled her newborn in her arms. Nurse Fatma sat next to her on the bed. They were talking about Servet's successful delivery.

Before leaving the tired but happy mother, Nurse Fatma asked, "Would you tell me the name you have chosen for your little girl?"

"My husband and I chose the name Bedia for her," replied Servet. "However, I'd also like to choose a second name. How about your name, Fatma?"

Pleasantly surprised, the head nurse smiled and shyly replied, "I'm flattered and greatly honored that you would consider naming your daughter after me."

Appreciating Fatma's devoted friendship and professional care, Servet said, "My dear friend, you have paid so much attention to me during my pregnancy that I will never forget you. Please, allow me the honor of naming her Fatma."

After Fatma had left the room, Servet gazed down at her baby lovingly. "Fatma Bedia," she whispered. "Welcome to my life."

A House in Disarray

Burhan was suddenly awakened by loud voices coming from various parts of the house. What he heard indicated to him that there was a serious argument going on between Ismet and his uncle. He also recognized the voice of Dursun, the nephew, who appeared to have gotten involved in the argument as well. It was still pitch dark. As he walked toward the door to listen to the ongoing argument, Burhan tripped over a small table; losing his balance, he fell on the wooden floor. As he struggled to get to his feet, the door to the family room was suddenly flung open. Ismet, looking like a ghost, stood with a gas lamp in his hand and shouted Burhan's name. Rushing into the room, he almost tripped over Burhan, who was struggling to stand up.

"Hurry up!" Ismet hollered. "We have to leave immediately! I had a fight with my nephew. We must leave this house. Let's go! I'll tell you all about it on the way."

When they were about to leave the house, Ismet's uncle, holding a towel tightly wrapped around his left arm, stopped them at the doorway. Ismet asked his uncle how bad his wound was. Burhan suddenly realized that what he had heard earlier had not just been an argument, but a bloody fight. Ismet's uncle, trying hard to keep a smile on his face, said that he had been able to stop the bleeding. He then asked Ismet how his leg was. Ignoring the question, Ismet quickly said good-bye to his uncle and dragged Burhan out of the house.

As they walked hurriedly up the hill toward the forest, Burhan noticed that Ismet was limping. He asked what happened to his leg. Ismet explained that he had a fight with his nephew early in the morning.

"Dursun had stabbed me in the upper part of my right leg. If not for my uncle jumping between us, Dursun would have stabbed me right in the belly. His knife cut my uncle's arm and went into my leg. I was then able to hit him hard right in his face, knocking him out cold. I tied him up before coming to wake you."

Burhan stopped walking and asked Ismet to explain what had caused the fight. Ismet grabbed Burhan's arm and told him that they couldn't afford to stop and talk. Holding Ismet's arm tightly to help him walk, Burhan asked again, "Why did Dursun want to kill you?"

"It's the other way around," replied Ismet. "I wanted to kill that bastard nephew of mine for being a snitch. After dinner, uncle told me it was Dursun who had betrayed me to the authorities. I asked what made him suspect Dursun. He told me that the morning after I had been taken away by the police, he heard Dursun talking to his wife. Unaware that my uncle was listening, they were discussing how good it was to get me, the traitor, out of the way. So last night after we left you to sleep, I asked Dursun to come into my room. I questioned him about what I had heard from my uncle. Then I tried to explain why I did what I did. He cut me short and said that regardless of the reasons, I was still a traitor. I lost control and attacked him with my knife. Dursun may not be able to walk well, but he has very strong arms. He took the knife away, hoping to finish me off. Thanks to my uncle, I'm still around."

Just as he finished his sentence, Ismet lost his balance and fell flat on his face. Burhan tried to help him get up. Ismet asked Burhan to find a wooden stick to help him walk. After a quick search,

Burhan found a fallen tree branch and brought it to Ismet. They sat for a few minutes, watching the sun rise. With the arrival of the light, Burhan noticed that Ismet's leg was wet with fresh blood. "My dear brother," he said. "You're badly wounded. You need medical attention. Let's go!"

They started to move toward the entrance to the forest. Before entering the forest, they paused to look down the hill at the charming Turkish-Albanian village. The sun was about to rise. They appreciated the orange tint of glistening sunlight reflecting on the dew-covered red-tiled roof tops. Suddenly, Ismet noticed a group of Ottoman soldiers at the edge of the village walking up the hill toward them. He pointed them out to Burhan. "They've seen us. They'll catch up with us in about fifteen minutes."

Recognizing the seriousness of the situation, Burhan grabbed Ismet's arm to get him to move faster, telling him that they were very close to the rendezvous point. "They're waiting for me up in the forest with horses," he explained. "We'll get away and get you some medical help."

A few minutes later they arrived at the spot where the Serbian nationalist soldiers were supposed to meet Burhan and take him back to the military garrison at Mitrovica. There was no one there. Frantic and frightened, Burhan started to curse. Ismet asked him to calm down. Not knowing what to do next, Burhan's mind was reeling. Ismet calmly told Burhan to move ahead and leave him behind. "I'll keep them busy for a while," he said. "That will give you the time and distance you need to make it back to the nationalist army quarters."

Burhan noticed that Ismet's leg was still bleeding profusely. "You know they'll kill you immediately," he said.

"Burhan, my brother," Ismet replied. "You have no choice in this matter. If we try to move together, and by some luck make it to the other side, we'll both be shot on the spot. Remember that you are wearing an Ottoman army uniform. My dear younger brother, I suggest you remove your uniform and gun, and give them to me. Keep your trousers; mine are too bloody for you to wear."

Without a word, Burhan removed his military coat, his shirt, and the Ottoman revolver that Commander Karaevitch had given him. He laid them on the ground, and then helped Ismet remove his overcoat and shirt and put on the Ottoman military coat. As he handed him the revolver, Burhan embraced Ismet and bid him farewell.

Ismet settled down under a large tree and put the revolver on the ground next to him. "The Ottoman soldiers will be here soon. Go away now! May the Lord help you with your mission."

As Burhan began to move away speedily, he heard Ismet yell, "Thank you brother, for the three exciting days you've added to my life."

The Wedding of Soul Mates

When the lieutenant was away on mission, Jemal usually slept in the house on the floor next to the kitchen stove. He was awakened by a loud knock on the door. "Who could be visiting us at this early hour?" he mumbled as he rose to his feet. He opened the door to welcome Colonel Husnu into the house.

Nurse Fatma walked into the entry hall to see who was calling at such an early hour of the morning. Shedding his overcoat, Colonel Husnu asked about Servet. After the nurse had told him that Servet was doing well, the colonel asked Fatma to acquire Servet Hanim's consent for a brief meeting to discuss some urgent matters. Before departing for Servet's room, Fatma asked Jemal to prepare a cup of tea for the colonel. A few minutes later, Servet, holding the baby in her arms cautiously entered the sitting room and sat on the divan.

After the usual exchange of respectful and courteous words, Colonel Husnu said, "Madam, I am very happy that you have given birth to a healthy little girl. A messenger was sent to Pristina last night to inform Lieutenant Avni. As you might already know, we are now in a state of military evacuation. During the next few days some of us must leave Yanyevo for Skopje. It will be a long and dangerous journey. Before I finalize the evacuation strategy, I would like to know when you will be strong enough to travel."

Servet, sitting upright and dignified, kept rocking the baby in her arms. "If necessary," she replied, "I can be ready to travel tomorrow. Please, let me know your plans as soon as you decide, Colonel."

Looking adoringly at the baby, Colonel Husnu said, "Such a beautiful little girl! I think we should move both of you to Skopje with the main evacuation convoy that is scheduled to depart the day after tomorrow. Please be ready. Jemal will provide all necessary assistance to your family during the evacuation. The trip may take three or four days, depending on the weather. Now, madam, with your permission, I must leave. God willing, you'll reach safety in Skopje within a few days."

"Colonel Husnu, before you leave my house," Servet calmly requested, "I would greatly appreciate it if you could tell me the chances of my ever being reunited with my husband."

This was exactly the type of question the colonel had wanted to avoid. He reached into the left inner pocket of his uniform and took out an envelope. "Madam, I almost forgot," he calmly said. "I received this from Lieutenant Avni a few days ago. He asked me to give it to you immediately after the birth of your child. As for your question, I honestly don't know the answer. Perhaps the answer is in the letter." After he handed the envelope to Servet, he quickly left the room.

Servet handed the baby to Fatma and asked the nurse to look after her for a short while. After Fatma's departure, Servet quietly sat on the divan for a long time before finding the courage to open the envelope. It was a long letter full of concerns and worries. It contained detailed instructions to her and Jemal regarding safety precautions during the evacuation. More importantly, the letter was also full of expressions about fatherhood. Avni had written that, by the time Servet read his letter, she would be a mother. As long as both mother and child were healthy, it didn't matter to him if the child was a boy or a girl. Avni then described the dangerous situation he was facing. He commented that only God could know if they would ever be together again. The letter continued with tender words of love and devotion and ended with the following paragraph:

My beautiful wife, I hope you have forgiven me for the insensitive and crude behavior that I very wrongly displayed on our wedding night. Soon, we might face the enemy on the battlefield. I don't know if I will survive the ordeal of the next few days. I do not want to leave this earth without letting you know that, since my shameful behavior on our wedding night, I have learned the true meaning of beauty. You, my dear wife, are the most beautiful, loving, and caring person I have ever known. Your true and everlasting beauty has been reflected through your expressions of love since the beginning of our time together. Miracles do happen. I pray that God's mercy and compassion will protect us all, and allow us to spend the rest of our lives together with our child. I should say 'our children'. God willing, we will have more.

Your loving husband Avni

Servet, crying silently, folded the letter and hugged it to her breast. In the silence of the early morning hours, she recalled her wedding. It had been more than three years since Avni's mother negotiated with Servet's mother about the possibility of marriage between their children. Servet had been barely fifteen years old when she was asked to serve tea to Avni's mother. Her future mother-in-law wanted to observe the future bride. Her mother instructed Servet to wear her best dress and put on a happy face to impress her future mother-in-law. Servet's mother thought a marriage proposal from the family of a young Ottoman army officer promised a secure future for her youngest daughter.

That very morning, while combing Servet's long blond hair, her mother had commented how beautiful her daughter looked with her sky-blue eyes and silky-smooth skin. She gleefully murmured, "I am certain the young lieutenant's mother will be impressed by your natural beauty."

Her mother was right; immediately after the usual tea ceremony and the lengthy informal discussions, an agreement was reached for further negotiations. Of course, nothing would proceed without approval from the young lieutenant.

Within a few weeks, Servet's parents received an offer of marriage between Avni and Servet. After formal discussions between the two families, an agreement of engagement and a date for the marriage was agreed upon. However, before the marriage could take place, Lieutenant Avni was ordered to the eastern front to join the military campaign organized against an anticipated Russian onslaught on the border. Both families agreed to postpone the wedding until his return.

Avni came back safely from the eastern front six months later. Unfortunately, during Avni's absence, Servet had contracted a nearly fatal case of small pox. She had survived the long illness, but her face had been permanently marred by the deep scars of the dreadful illness. Her parents decided to keep her ailment and the resultant damage to her face a secret in order to retain the opportunity to wed their now ill-fated daughter.

The wedding ceremony and festivities lasted all day and into the evening. Avni and Servet were led to the bedroom for the consummation of their marriage. They were finally alone in the beautifully decorated wedding bedroom. Servet, petrified with fear by the possibility of Avni's rejection, was almost at the point of a nervous breakdown. Barely able to catch her breath, she stood in the middle of the room and stared at Avni through the silk lace scarf covering her face.

Avni, awkwardly and nervously, approached Servet. Expecting to see the beauty that had been described to him by his mother, he reached toward her face to lift the silk covering. As the veil was slowly lifted away from her face, Servet felt weak and sick to her stomach. She closed her eyes and held her breath.

Staring at the pale and scarred face of Servet, Avni recoiled in shock. Finding his voice at last, he shouted, "You are not the woman who was described to me! You are not and cannot be my wife!"

Servet closed her eyes. She heard Avni's boots pound heavily across the bedroom floor and a violent slamming of the door as he rushed out of the room. She gathered that he had stormed downstairs where some of the family members were still enjoying the wedding festivities. Servet slowly moved toward the bed, where she collapsed. Covering her face with her hands, she cried her heart out until she fell asleep from exhaustion.

More than a month passed before Avni sent Servet a message that he wanted to meet her. Servet was surprised to receive such a request. Countless unpleasant and fruitless meetings had taken place between the elders of both families to find a solution to this tragic situation. It was now up to Avni to either accept or dissolve the marriage. When Avni heard about Servet's terrible and life-threatening bout with small pox, he decided to meet with her before making his final decision.

At the home of a wealthy relative on the outskirts of the city of Izmit, a private lunch was arranged for the two of them. Servet welcomed Avni graciously as if nothing had happened. They ate and conversed for a long time. Avni asked her to walk with him in the beautiful gardens of the old Ottoman mansion. They strolled and talked for hours. It was then that Avni noticed Servet's beautiful blue eyes and her long, blond hair. He observed how she moved with pride and dignity, and spoke eloquently on all matters of life. Most importantly, Avni was impressed by her intelligence and the inquisitiveness of her mind.

Two weeks later, Avni and Servet took the morning train to Istanbul to consummate their marriage at the famous Pera Palace Hotel. A few months later, when Avni was reassigned as the supply officer at the military medical unit in Yanyevo, they moved to Kosovo.

A Proud Father

It was barely dawn when the Yanyevo unit began the strategic move toward the hills northeast of Kosovo Polje, the Field of Blackbirds. Lieutenant Avni led the convoy toward its new location. Within a few hours, the convoy arrived at the world-famous battleground. The infantry and cavalry troops were ordered to stop and rest.

Dismounting, Avni spoke pensively, "Mehmetali, this is the famous battlefield where the Serbian king and the Ottoman sultan lost their lives."

Handing the reins to the staff sergeant, Avni asked Mehmetali to follow him. They walked between the burial markers on the battleground. Avni told Mehmetali that in those days soldiers who were killed in battle had been buried on the ground where they had fallen.

"Lieutenant, where are we going?" Mehmetali asked anxiously.

Avni raised his right arm to point at a small rundown mausoleum in the middle of the battlefield. They quietly walked to the building and stood in front of it.

"The day before the battle, while receiving an emissary of the Serbian king, Sultan Murad was assassinated at this location. His internal organs, including his heart, are buried here. The rest of the sultan's body was taken to Bursa, former capital of the empire, and laid to rest next to his father. Let us pray for the soul of the great sultan and for ourselves, so that we will be able to defend this land and the five hundred years of Ottoman heritage built upon it."

As they were finishing their prayers, someone shouted the lieutenant's name. Mehmetali turned around and noticed the staff sergeant and a soldier hurriedly rushing toward them.

Avni inquired, "Who is the young soldier running beside the sergeant?"

"I think he's an infantryman who is also named Avni," replied Mehmetali. "He is the young recruit whom I sent back to Yanyevo with your letters to the colonel."

Avni realized that the young soldier was bringing him news from Yanyevo. His heart was pounding and he felt dizzy. He held onto the mausoleum's frame, closed his eyes and prayed for good news. It felt like a very long time before he heard Mehmetali asking him if he was all right. He opened his eyes and saw the young Yanyevo recruit standing in front of him, waiting for permission to speak. Lieutenant Avni ordered the young soldier to deliver the message. The young man explained that he had no written message.

"Sir, I was instructed to tell you that you now are the father of a healthy baby girl. Jemal asked me to tell you that your wife is doing very well."

Avni knew that the young man had ridden his horse all night and a great part of the day to give him the good news. He thanked the young soldier profusely and repeatedly. Before dismissing him, Avni asked the young soldier, "What do you know about the evacuation to Skopje?"

The young soldier told Avni that there were preparations for the evacuation, but he did not know for sure when the actual move to Skopje would begin. Avni ordered Mehmetali and the young soldier to return to camp and rest. He waited until they had reached the edge of the old battleground and then sat down on the ground. As he leaned back on the mausoleum's wall, he offered a lengthy prayer and thanked the Lord for the blessed news. "Welcome into my life, my little Bedia," he murmured.

Avni's Father in the Sultan's Court

By late afternoon, the Yanyevo detachment had established a temporary camp at the eastern end of the Ottoman defense front. The detachment was still a day's journey from their assigned position. That evening, Mehmetali made sure that a special meal was served to Lieutenant Avni. All the soldiers greeted him respectfully and congratulated him on his fatherhood. Even the well-respected hodja of the third army regiment visited Avni to give his personal greetings. They talked for a long time. Mehmetali, who served tea to both, noticed that the hodja kept referring to Avni's father as "the honorable one."

After the hodja's departure, Mehmetali brought Avni a fresh cup of tea and respectfully inquired, "Sir, why did the hodja refer to your father as 'the honorable one'?"

With a joyous look on his face, Avni answered, "Mehmetali, it's a long story. Go and get a cup of tea for yourself and join me. I'll tell you all about it."

As he sipped the last drops of tea from his cup, Avni began the story of his father, who once had been a deputy mufti in the sultan's Dolmabahce palace in Istanbul.

"My father, Ali, was born in the city of Erzurum during the reign of the great Sultan Abdul Mejid. With the support of the local religious authority, my grandfather, a prominent and wealthy shopkeeper, placed my father in a local religious school to become a Muslim scholar. After successfully completing his studies, he attended the most prestigious religious academy in the empire, located in Istanbul. Before graduation, he went back to Erzurum to marry my mother. Together, they returned to Istanbul. A few years later, because of his famous Friday lectures at the mosque of the Dolmabahce Palace, he became a member of the palace clergy. He occasionally delivered a Friday prayer sermon in the mosque where the members the royal family prayed. My older brother and sister were born during that prosperous period in the family history. The royal family noticed my father's lectures and appreciated his elegant demeanor at meetings concerning religious affairs. They also took note of his daring ideas about maintaining religious properties through public contributions. Sultan Abdul Hamid particularly appreciated my father's financial genius and promoted him to the rank of deputy mufti of the Dolmabahce palace. Mufti Ali Efendi, as he was called after his promotion, became a favorite of the sultan's court."

After a long pause, Avni continued with his father's story. "Yet one day, my father made the greatest mistake of his life. As in most places of power, the seraglio was full of intrigues and schemes of all sorts. A junior prince named Ahmed, son of the sultan's deceased sister, had fallen desperately in love with the young daughter of a harem concubine who was still held in favor by the sultan. One day, Prince Ahmed, who was in his mid-twenties, approached my father. He requested assistance in acquiring the sultan's permission to marry this young girl of the harem, named Feride, who was barely fifteen years old. My father's first and correct reaction was to tell Prince Ahmed to approach the sultan through his own royal connections. Prince Ahmed confided that he had already tried that approach, but his request had not been considered important enough to bring to the attention of the sultan. My father then asked the prince if he had tried to reach the sultan through the mother of his sweetheart. The prince informed my father that Zeynep Hanim, the mother of the young girl, had already agreed to the proposed marriage and had obtained the sultan's informal agreement. The young prince then asked my father to conduct the marriage ceremony."

Avni gratefully accepted a fresh cup of tea from Mehmetali. Taking a few sips, he continued the story. "While Mufti Ali Efendi's rational mind was telling him not to get involved, his heart went out to the young prince, whom he had known since childhood. Within a few days, a secret marriage ceremony took place in one of the hidden courtrooms far from the daily activities of the palace. The young prince was dressed in royal attire, and the young girl appeared in a traditional wedding dress, covered from head to toe, including her face. Mufti Ali Efendi could see through the thin lace covering her face that the young girl was beautiful. After completing the ceremony, my father asked the prince where they were planning to settle. The prince said they would leave immediately for Kutahya in Anatolia, where he would soon become the deputy governor of the city. My father then asked the prince to keep this wedding ceremony a secret for the rest of his life. It was kept so for quite a while, almost two years."

Mehmetali impatiently inquired, "Tell me what happened two years later."

Smiling broadly, Avni said, "One day, unexpectedly, the disappearance of Feride came to the sultan's attention. The sultan was informed that rumors circulating in the harem suggested that Feride had married Prince Ahmed. They were thought to be living in Kutahya. The sultan asked who had married them without his consent. He was told that Mufti Ali Efendi had performed the service two years earlier. The sultan was furious. He first banished his concubine, Zeynep Hanim, to a remote part of Anatolia. He then demoted the young prince to third-class officer, and later, moved him and his wife Feride to a godforsaken corner of the empire, somewhere in the Saharan Desert."

Taking a couple of sips of his tea, Avni continued, "The sultan then summoned my father, demanding an explanation. After hearing his side of the story, the sultan ordered him thrown in prison. As my father waited miserably in his jail cell, he knew he might lose his head. A few weeks later, the chief barrister of the sultan brought the matter of my father to the attention of the royal court. The sultan asked the birthplace of my father. When the sultan heard that my father had been born in the city of Erzurum in eastern Anatolia, the sultan ordered him and his family banished to Erzurum for the rest of his life. A couple of years later, I was born on a cold wintry night. Many years later, after I had finished middle school, my father, using his earlier connections, was able to enroll me in the Kuleli military high school in Istanbul. Immediately after I had graduated from the war academy, a constitutional government was established in Istanbul. As the powers of the sultan became somewhat limited during that time, my father risked moving the family to Izmit, a town eighty kilometers east of Istanbul. That is where my future wife, Servet, and her family lived."

Charmed by the story of Avni's father, Mehmetali warmly thanked the lieutenant and then graciously asked permission to leave for guard duty.

VENGEANCE AND COMPASSION

The Eighth of January: Burhan in Prison

Just as the sun was about to set behind a bend in the river, Burhan reached the outskirts of Mitrovica. He noticed a group of nationalist soldiers approaching him. One of the soldiers shouted at Burhan to stop. Immediately he stopped walking and waited for the soldiers to reach him. One of the soldiers, apparently the head of the group, ordered Burhan to raise his hands. The soldier searched Burhan's body for weapons. Finding none, he asked for identification papers. Burhan told the soldier that he had no papers because he was returning from a special mission to Pristina. The soldier stared at Burhan for a long moment before suddenly kicking him in the groin. Coldly watching Burhan curl into a fetal position on the ground, he ordered another soldier to tie Burhan's hands behind his back.

A few minutes later, Burhan was dragged into the Mitrovica militia headquarters for interrogation and placed in a sparsely furnished room. Looking out the window into the courtyard below, he felt cold, humid air blowing through the broken windowpane. It was a very chilly and wet evening. Shivering, he wondered how to make his interrogators believe him. Eventually, a young militia officer entered the room and ordered Burhan to sit on the other side of the desk.

The officer asked him where he had been going when he was arrested. Burhan explained that he had been returning from a special mission to Pristina.

"Under whose authority was this special mission?" the officer asked Burhan.

"I received my orders directly from Commander Karaevitch," replied Burhan. He then asked the officer to summon Lieutenant Michailovitch to confirm his story. The request was ignored; it was obvious to Burhan that the officer did not believe him.

Over the following long hours, Burhan was questioned by several other officers. Finally, the last officer ordered the guards to take him to jail. At the entry to the large prison cell, Burhan hesitated and was kicked in the rear by the guard so forcefully that he sprawled onto his face on the crowded chamber's dirt floor. He slowly rose to his feet, wiping dirt from his face.

A young man came up to Burhan and asked, in Serbo-Croatian, who he was. Before answering, Burhan glanced quickly around the cell. He saw many men of various ages crowded into the cold, damp room. To Burhan, most of the jailed men looked like Turkish-Albanian thugs. His intuition told him that if they knew who he really was, they would kill him immediately. He decided to pretend he was an Albanian villager. He told the young man that when the nationalists had attacked his village south of Mitrovica, he had been taken hostage. In order to prevent further inquiry, Burhan quickly asked him why he was in prison.

The young man first introduced himself, and then asked Burhan his name. Burhan shook the hand of this new acquaintance, who was named Memodagic, and asked him where he was from.

"In this cell all of us are from Sanjak and other southern Serbian provinces," Memodagic replied. "We are Slavic Muslims. There are eighteen of us here in this cell. For many weeks we've been under interrogation. In Serbia, many of us fought on the side of the Serbian nationalists. After many battles, most of the Slavic Muslims were arrested as traitors."

Burhan coldly responded, "You must have done something to be identified as a traitor."

"Most of us are being punished for not agreeing to kill defenseless civilians," answered Memodagic. "Some will be executed for refusing to murder Muslim prisoners."

"What do you mean by murder of Muslim prisoners? I thought nationalists never took prisoners."

"Not true. The nationalist army occasionally makes prisoners of soldiers who surrender or who are slightly wounded. First, the prisoners are tortured until they give information. Then they're executed in the cruelest way. If you're interested, you're welcome to watch the show from the cell window tomorrow morning."

After a long pause, the young prisoner, who had been staring intently into Burhan's face, loudly remarked, "It's very strange that they put you, an Albanian villager, in here with us. I don't think you are telling us the truth."

Burhan suddenly felt panicky; how could he have known that the guards would throw him into a cell full of Slavic Muslims?

He quickly responded to Memodagic's inquiry. "I thought you were a group of Albanian prisoners. To protect myself, I told you that I'm an Albanian. Actually, I'm a Montenegrin Muslim. Like you, I'm under suspicion for being a traitor."

Memodagic, now joined by two other young men, continued to stare intently into Burhan's eyes. "I don't think you are either an Albanian or a Muslim Montenegrin. I think you are a Serbian or a Croat. Take down your trousers; we'll see if you are really a Muslim."

Burhan knew he had no choice but to expose his penis to prove that he was circumcised. He quickly lowered his trousers and underwear, exposing himself to the scrutiny of the three young prisoners. Memodagic loudly declared to the other prisoners that the newcomer's circumcised penis had spoken; it had revealed the truth.

As the inmates roared with laughter, Memodagic turned to Burhan and explained, "There are no shared jail cells with Albanian or Ottoman prisoners. After an Ottoman or Albanian soldier is caught, he is usually interrogated, tortured, and then placed in a wretched isolation cell. A day or two later, the prisoner is executed in the courtyard. As I said before, you can watch tomorrow morning. I think several Ottoman soldiers, a few local Turks, and some Albanian thugs are scheduled for execution."

The Ninth of January: Bayonet Training

The remainder of the night was quiet but uncomfortable for Burhan. He could not sleep, thinking constantly about his father and Ismet.

When the first rays of sun illuminated the dark, smelly cell, Memodagic walked toward the window. He pointed to the center of the courtyard where a dozen thick, wooden poles had been buried in the ground approximately one meter apart. "That is where the prisoners are executed," he said. "It's a training ground for new recruits." With a humorless smile on his face, he continued, "Here they are. Go ahead and watch; I've seen it several times already."

Burhan moved closer to the window to see what was happening in the courtyard. Twelve men of various ages were waiting to be lashed to the poles. A few of the prisoners wore Ottoman uniforms, but most were in civilian clothes. Two military guards brought a tall, slender Ottoman soldier next to the pole. They pressed his back straight against the pole and tied his hands at the back. They then pulled his legs apart and tied them tightly to the pole. One by one, all the prisoners were tied to the poles in the same manner. Burhan noticed that the courtyard was now full of nationalist soldiers. He counted: there were exactly forty-eight. He wondered why so many would be needed for a firing squad.

The commanding officer ordered the soldiers into formations of twelve lines with four soldiers in each line. The officer then asked the soldiers to prepare their bayonets and line up approximately ten meters across from each pole. When the soldiers were ready, the officer raised his hand and, after a long pause, bellowed, "Charge!" Twelve newly recruited soldiers with fixed bayonets charged toward the twelve doomed prisoners tied to the poles. Burhan could detect shades of fear and horror on the faces of the prisoners whose eyes were not covered. Upon reaching the body of the prisoners, each soldier forcefully thrust his bayonet into the midsection of the prisoner he was facing. As they twisted their rifles to cause maximal damage to the internal organs, the soldiers pulled their bayonets out of the screaming prisoners. Then they moved behind the poles to allow the second column of soldiers to charge against the already mauled and bleeding bodies of the doomed prisoners.

Sickened by the cruelty of the execution, Burhan lowered his head to look at Memodagic, who was sitting on the floor right below him. "But why?" he asked.

Coldly, Memodagic answered, "It saves bullets and gets the new recruits ready for battle."

Burhan, shaken and nauseated by what he had witnessed, slowly slid down to the floor next to Memodagic.

"What ails you my friend?" Memodagic asked. Without waiting for Burhan's answer, he continued, "This is nothing compared to what I, or most of us in this cell, have been exposed to during the past few months. At the beginning, our nonparticipation during the deadly attacks on unarmed Muslim civilians was ignored. But later, we were ordered to participate in acts of violence against the Muslim civilians, mostly Turks and Albanians. When we refused, the officer-in-charge explained to us that these violent attacks were part of a strategy to scare the Muslims into leaving. He said that if these attacks on Muslim communities resulted in voluntary evacuations, there would be no need for further violence or killing. Based on this warped rationale, almost all the Serbian officers ignored the cruel and inhuman activities of their troops. This resulted in most soldiers raping and killing many young Muslim girls. As part of the ploy, a few of the Turkish men and the raped young girls were allowed to escape so they could spread fear in the hearts of Muslims in areas still under Ottoman control."

Burhan, staring blankly ahead, told Memodagic of the similar situations he had witnessed during several battles. "But I never thought that it was a strategic plan to force local Muslims to move away and vacate their towns and villages. I think using human beings for bayonet practice is an outrageously inhumane thing to do."

Memodagic calmly responded, "To the nationalists, these targets are not human beings; they are just enemies to be destroyed. It's a common military conditioning tactic to desensitize the newly recruited troops."

A few hours later, Lieutenant Michailovitch stood outside the communal cell door and identified Burhan to the guard. As he heard the door open, Burhan looked up and saw the lieutenant. The husky prison guard rudely ordered Burhan to get up and follow him. Burhan turned to Memodagic and wished him good luck. The young Slavic Muslim, appearing sad, told Burhan that it would soon be over and that he would meet his maker. Realizing that Memodagic assumed him to be on his way to execution, Burhan gave Memodagic a hug. As he turned around to leave the smelly, cold prison cell, Burhan replied, "Sooner or later we all meet our maker."

Staring at Burhan, Lieutenant Michailovitch's first comment was that he looked and smelled like rotting fruit. Burhan responded, "I feel worse than I look. It's been a tough ordeal indeed. What happened? Why didn't the special unit meet me at the rendezvous point?"

Michailovitch answered stoically, "The special unit was attacked by an Ottoman infantry group and was delayed in arriving at the meeting point. When they finally arrived, the soldiers found the mutilated body of an Ottoman military police sergeant. They assumed that you had been killed by the Ottoman soldiers. When I received a note from the officer who interrogated you about your story of being on a special mission ordered by Commander Karaevitch, I decided to check the prison to see if you were there. Aren't you glad to see me? Tomorrow you'll meet Karaevitch and brief him on your important discoveries. You smell terrible. Please, take a bath and get a new uniform."

Burhan replied without hesitation, "I don't care how bad I smell! I'm starving. First, take me to the kitchen."

Bad News from Home

The dispatcher from the Skopje regional Military Headquarters entered the Yanyevo administrative office as Lieutenant Nihad was reviewing plans for the coming evacuation. Dropping the bag of mail on the floor and the envelope of orders on the desk, the dispatcher asked the lieutenant for the mailbag that was to be taken back to Skopje headquarters. As he handed over the single envelope from the colonel, Lieutenant Nihad explained to the dispatcher that there was no more mail to be sent because almost everyone would soon be evacuated to Skopje.

Once the dispatcher left the room, the lieutenant called the office sergeant to open the general mail bag. "After inspecting each and every envelope, distribute the mail to those staff present. Mail for staff at the front should be sent to Pristina, to be distributed later."

The office sergeant returned an hour later and handed an envelope to Lieutenant Nihad. "Sir," he said wearily, "we received personal mail for Jemal. I think you should read it."

Lieutenant Nihad knew from experience that the sergeant's request usually meant bad news from home. The letter was from Jemal's uncle, informing him that his wife, Aisha, had passed away. The letter explained that she had died from pneumonia. Selim, his son, was being cared for by Jemal's mother and the rest of the family. Lieutenant Nihad remembered Jemal telling a touching anecdote around a campfire one evening that his wife came from a courageous family. Her grandfather had served in the Ottoman forces for many years before he died in 1877 fighting the Russians in Bulgaria. Jemal said that his wife, Aisha, wanted to send their son Selim to military school so that he would follow the grandfather's footsteps. *Losing his wife will break Jemal's heart*, Lieutenant Nihad thought. He then instructed the sergeant that the contents of the letter should be kept confidential until they had reached Skopje. Nihad had no intention of telling Jemal about his wife's death just before their departure for Skopje. He knew that if Jemal survived the ordeal of evacuation he would then be honorably discharged from the military and repatriated to his hometown, Sivas. Lieutenant Nihad decided it would be best if Jemal learned about his wife's death directly from his family. Earlier, he had asked Colonel Husnu's permission to assign Jemal to peripheral security duties during the evacuation. Colonel Husnu had not consented, and had ordered

Nihad to assign Jemal to assist Lieutenant Avni's wife and child during the evacuation. Nihad did not approve, in principle, of the special attention given to Lieutenant Avni's family. Now, however, he felt that this assignment offered the best chance of survival for Jemal. Nihad ordered the sergeant to summon Jemal.

His talk with the lieutenant completed, Jemal walked out of the warm office into the cold, snow-covered streets of Yanyevo. He felt good about his assignment to care for Lieutenant Avni's family. This would be his final duty before he was discharged from the military. During the past year and a half, the lieutenant and his wife had been good to him. They had treated him with care and consideration, and because of Jemal's good military service record, the lieutenant had officially recommended him for an early discharge. He would soon be on his way home.

Happy and content, Jemal entered the house with a grin and merrily said good morning to Servet. He briefed her on the preparations for the next morning's departure to Skopje. Noticing that Jemal was jovial, Servet asked him what good news he had received. Jemal, still smiling, responded, "My dear madam, thanks to you and the lieutenant, upon reaching Skopje I'll leave for home and be on my way to Sivas."

The Tenth of January: Contrition

The next day before sunrise, the muezzin's call for prayer awoke Jemal from a deep sleep. He completed his morning prayers and left the house for the stables, thankful that his request for a mule and cart for the family's travel had been approved by Lieutenant Nihad. He had worked hard the previous day building a separate section in the cart for Servet and the newborn, one that would offer both privacy and protection from the harsh winter weather. He led the mule from the stable and harnessed it to the cart. After he had perched himself at the edge of the cart, Jemal watched the emerging light of dawn break over the ridge of the narrow valley through which the main road to Yanyevo passed. Feeling snowflakes landing on his forehead, he took his wool army hat out of his coat pocket and placed it on his head.

The scenery suddenly reminded Jemal of a disturbing incident he had hoped never to recall. It had happened exactly two years before, during the eerie quiet of dawn. This morning's cold breeze and swirling snowflakes reminded Jemal of those high hills in northern Thrace near the Bulgarian border. There, in self-defense, he had taken a man's life. That had been his first and only killing. Just before dawn, while he was standing guard, an advance Bulgarian infantry unit had unexpectedly attacked the Ottoman border defense posts. The initial bayonet charge quickly turned into hand-to-hand combat. One young enemy soldier attempted to thrust his bayonet into the middle of Jemal's torso. He remembered the handsome face of the young man who couldn't have been more than seventeen years old.

As if in slow motion, Jemal had seen the shiny, sharp blade moving toward his belly. Instinctively, to protect himself, Jemal moved to his right, and swung his left arm downward to block the blade that was about to enter his abdomen. He felt the blade pierce the flesh right below his elbow and enter the upper part of his left thigh. He then swung the long infantry knife in his right hand toward the young man's midsection. The knife entered the Bulgarian soldier's soft belly, ripping his guts and tearing his internal organs. Like two ballet dancers embracing each other in the final notes of a symphony, they fell, almost gracefully, to the snow-covered ground.

After a few seconds of silence, Jemal heard the young man scream. The mortally wounded soldier pulled his legs up in a fetal position, his head falling heavily on Jemal's chest. Jemal freed his right hand from the handle of the long knife pinned in the belly of the young man and brought his arm over the head of the twisted body that leaned on his chest. He then locked his arm around the young Bulgarian soldier's neck and squeezed with all his strength. The soldier's struggles slowly weakened and Jemal felt the final tremors of death. The eyes of the young Bulgarian, bulging wide, slowly glazed over. Still holding the dead man in his arms, Jemal began to feel excruciating pain from the deep wound in his thigh. He knew his only chance of survival depended on in his comrades' ability to repel the enemy. Otherwise, the surviving Bulgarian soldiers would cut him to pieces. The fighting still raged on all around him. So as not to be noticed by the enemy soldiers still fighting on all sides of him, he closed his eyes as if dead. Shortly afterward, he fell into a deep sleep.

When Jemal woke up, a couple of medics were preparing him for the journey to the hospital in Edirne. One of the medics, noticing Jemal's return to consciousness, smiled at him. He told Jemal that they'd had a hard time separating him from his Bulgarian friend.

Jemal had spent more than a month in the regional military hospital in Edirne before being transferred to the supplies management unit in Yanyevo.

The Convoy to Skopje

Servet interrupted Jemal's reminiscence. She opened the house door to look for Jemal who was sitting on the edge of the cart next to the stable; he appeared to be asleep. Servet called his name and asked him to carry her bags to the cart. Jemal jumped to his feet and pulled the mule toward the house. In a few minutes, the cart was loaded. They were ready to join the main evacuation convoy at the town square.

Servet returned to the house to bring little Bedia out to the cart. Holding the swaddled infant in her arms, she slowly walked through each room, reliving the good memories of her first home. In the middle of the bedroom, with her baby in her arms, she prayed for a safe journey for herself and her child, and for the safety of her husband.

Outside, still holding Bedia firmly in her arms, Servet settled into the cart. She was impressed with the alterations Jemal had made. The cart with huge wooden wheels was enclosed above as well as on all four sides with heavy canvas. There was a narrow opening at the front and back through which she could enter and exit. Several containers of basic supplies were carefully stacked behind the covered passenger area.

As he steadied the young mule by its muzzle, Jemal asked Servet if she was ready to move. Receiving Servet's reply, he pulled the mule onto the road.

Accompanied by the creaking sounds of the old wooden axle, the cart slowly began moving toward the town square. A few minutes later, it reached the tail end of the evacuation convoy. Opening the front canvas cover of the cart, Servet looked out to see what was going on. They were at the top of the hill facing the road to the main square. She observed that there were many open carts full of wounded soldiers toward the front of the convoy. There was also a long line of armed soldiers on foot and on horseback. As the cart passed the mosque in the main square, she saw Colonel Husnu on the stone stairway leading to the main entrance of the mosque. He stood at attention, a silent statue covered with snowflakes. As Servet's cart passed in front of him, the colonel raised both arms to wave, shouting, "Have a safe journey. God protect all of you!"

The convoy snaked slowly toward the southeastern end of the valley and the open plains of southern Kosovo.

Burhan's Report

Commander Karaevitch warmly welcomed Burhan to his office. After exchanging firm handshakes, he said, "You owe me a revolver, young man. But I'm glad you have returned safely. Lieutenant Michailovitch told me that our local informer sacrificed his life for you. We owe him gratitude for his heroism. Now tell me, what have you discovered during your daring mission behind the Ottoman defensive lines?"

Burhan thanked the commander for his warm welcome. He then asked a favor on behalf of Ismet's family. "During the coming battles," he began, "is it possible to provide security for the collaborator's family, so that no harm will come to them? Also, can they retain their property after we conquer their village?"

Karaevitch swiftly replied, "You have my word; his family will be protected. I'll make sure the members of his family remain both healthy and wealthy."

Burhan then told the commander that the Ottoman defensive fortifications were impressive. He deliberately exaggerated the strength of the Ottoman army, particularly the capacity of the artillery units located around the defensive lines. He falsely pointed out on the map two possible spearhead positions where the Ottomans were prepared to counterattack. He told the commander that one spearhead position was located near the northwest end of the Kosovo Polje defense line, and the other was at the northeast end of the Pristina defense line toward Pudujevo.

Karaevitch was surprised and asked for further explanations. They talked for a long time, occasionally pointing and marking certain locations on the maps. When the discussions were completed,

Karaevitch offered Burhan a cigarette and announced that he had been promoted to the rank of sergeant.

Burhan thanked the commander, saluted smartly, and asked to be excused. As he was leaving the room, he overheard Karaevitch order the postponement of the general attack until necessary adjustments had been made to troop and artillery positions. Hearing this, he smiled; the misinformation he had delivered to the commander might cause the conflict to end in a stalemate or, at least, delay the inevitable victory by the nationalists. Such a delay would give the Ottoman army additional time to withdraw to southern Kosovo.

That will definitely be the end result, he thought, *if my father follows my suggestion and reports what I told him to his commanding officer.*

Outside the command center, Burhan saw Lieutenant Michailovitch waiting to see the commander. The lieutenant asked Burhan to wait for him until his meeting with Commander Karaevitch had been completed. "I expect," he cheerfully said, "the commander will ask us to conduct a very thrilling mission soon."

Michailovitch returned a while later and informed Burhan that Karaevitch had ordered a special intelligence mission to begin immediately. "Be ready to depart early tomorrow morning," he ordered.

"Where are we going?" asked Burhan.

To make sure that no one around would hear his reply, Michailovitch whispered, "To the Gypsy camp north of Mitrovica."

Mehmetali's Revelation

Avni, completing his noon prayers, walked out of the temporary masjid and sat down to pull on his boots. Mehmetali came next to him and asked, "How did you like the hodja's lecture today, Lieutenant?"

"I did not like it at all," replied Avni. "It does not make sense anymore to become a sacrificial lamb for the empire and the faith. For decades we have been fighting in the Balkans for a lost cause. We've become the enemy in our own backyard."

As they walked toward the mess tent for a bite to eat, Mehmetali responded to Avni's depressing comments, "Lieutenant, with your permission, sir, what you have said may apply to Turks and other Ottoman nationalities who settled in Kosovo after the Ottomans took possession of Balkan territories. Please remember, sir, we Albanians have been here since the beginning of time."

"Mehmetali, I fully agree with your point," Avni firmly replied. "But please, do not forget that Kosovo has also been our home for five centuries. The empire's various ethnicities and religions coexisted with tolerance and understanding for more than half a millennium. Now, the arrival of nationalism has made everybody fight for a homeland of their own. It now appears that nobody wants the Turks or the Muslims in Europe. If we lose this coming battle, a new Ottoman state boundary may be established at the Kosovo-Macedonia border. Only God knows for how long we will be able to hold on to the remaining European part of the empire."

Avni stopped walking and turned to Mehmetali. "Before the prayers today," he tensely said, "the respected hodja was lecturing that the righteousness and power of Allah are on our side because we are defending our country. I'm not in agreement with his wishful thinking. In the Balkans, I think, we are no longer in our own country. It is very strange indeed for us to defend a piece of land where we are neither accepted nor respected as people who were once a part of this land. So, to whom should Kosovo belong? I think it should rightfully belong to all the people who live on the land now: Turks, Albanians, Croats, Serbs, Armenians, Greeks, Gypsies, and Jews. If we lose the coming battle, the Turks will be forced to leave Kosovo, just as happened in Bosnia-Herzegovina and Serbia. Those who remain in Kosovo will fight each other to the bitter end to create an ethnically purified land of their own."

Mehmetali, noticing that the lieutenant was getting stressed, asked for permission to get tea for both of them. He returned with two cups of freshly brewed tea and some dried apricots. Sitting across from Avni, he apprehensively said, "Lieutenant, if you promise that what I'm about to tell you will not result in any harm to me, I'd like to confide in you."

Avni, looking at his old friend, asked him, "What're you talking about?"

Mehmetali repeated his appeal. "I'm about to tell you something extremely important," he said emphatically. "Please tell me that you will trust me and cause me no harm."

Avni was becoming both curious and nervous about the conversation.

"You don't need to worry. No one will harm you for giving me information. Please, tell me, what's it about?"

Now relaxed, Mehmetali told Avni of his chance encounter with Burhan three days earlier. "My son was apparently on an intelligence mission," Mehmetali said. "He was collecting information on Ottoman troop movements and artillery locations. He informed me that the enemy has received large supplies of military hardware and a sizeable contingent of new volunteers from the European support group. In addition, thousands of well-trained and well-equipped Austro-Hungarian infantry soldiers wearing nationalist uniforms have joined the Serbian army."

There was a long period of silence before Avni spoke. "Mehmetali," he said. "What you are telling me requires evidence. How do we know that what Burhan told you was true? Even if we take the information at face value and tell the commanding officer, he might not believe it. If he did choose to believe it, he would have to place you, possibly both of us, in custody for further questioning."

Avni abruptly got up. Before leaving the tent, he said, "I wish you had never told me!"

That evening Avni was unable to sleep. He was deeply disturbed by Mehmetali's sudden revelation of confidential military information. If true, it could mean a disastrous military situation for the Ottoman defensive positions. The presence of regular Austro-Hungarian troops among the nationalist infantry would create serious military setbacks for the Ottoman army. The well-trained and seasoned soldiers of the Viennese empire could win the battle for the nationalists. Given the sensitive nature of the information, Avni considered revealing it to the intelligence unit at Pristina Military Headquarters. Throughout the long night, he wondered how he could pass the information to the proper authorities without getting himself or Mehmetali in trouble. Draping his blanket over his army coat, Avni walked out of his tent. He sat on a stool to watch the sunrise. It was very calm and quiet outside. For a while, he watched the dry snowflakes gently float through the air and slowly blanket everything in and around the camp, making the sleeping ground of the slumbering warriors appear quite peaceful.

Half an hour later, when it stopped snowing, Avni watched the first rays of light appear from the high hills behind his tent. From the vantage point of his tent, he felt the warm, mellow light of dawn on his face. Shading his eyes with his hand, he focused on the remarkable scenery before him: hundreds of snow-covered tents stretching away to the outskirts of Kosovo Polje, the Field of Blackbirds. All these poor resting souls were about to face a formidable enemy that would eliminate every one of them without mercy. He prayed for the Lord's guidance to make a just and proper decision soon, and the courage to act on such a decision.

Deciding on what to do, he slowly got on his feet. *Neither Mehmetali nor I matter now,* he thought. *If we don't speak out and report what we know, we will be destroyed by the enemy. If we do speak out, we will probably die at the hands of our own people. Either way, both of us are doomed. It would be best to report what we know and accept the consequences.*

He returned to his tent and lay down on his cot for a few minutes' sleep before the bugler woke the camp.

The Eleventh of January: Jemal Meets Aisha

A cold but sunny morning marked the beginning of the second day of the evacuation convoy to Skopje. Jemal busied himself making a fire to prepare tea. After putting the kettle over the fast-burning dry wood, he walked toward the mule to wipe the snowflakes from the animal's back. He could hear Servet murmuring to her little daughter in the cart. He had emptied the cart the previous evening, just before nightfall. Inside, he had laid out a mattress heaped with blankets for Servet and Bedia. Jemal hoped that the mother and child had passed the night in reasonable comfort.

Descending from the cart, Servet asked Jemal if the tea was ready. Glancing at the fire, he answered, "Madam, it'll be ready soon." A few minutes later, Jemal returned to the cart with a cup of steaming hot tea. He found Servet sitting on the backboard between the two large wheels. He handed her the cup of tea, then went back for some food.

Servet took the plate of bread and cheese Jemal had brought, and asked him to have a cup of tea and join her for breakfast. Holding the hot cup between his palms, Jemal leaned against the large wooden cartwheel.

"Thank you, madam," he said. "I've already had my breakfast. I guess little Bedia is still asleep."

"Yes, she is," replied Servet. After a moment of silence, she continued, "Jemal, could there be any threat to our safety during this trip?"

Jemal was well aware that he could not deceive Servet with inaccurate statements. "I'm not quite sure how to answer your question, madam," he said shyly. "Honestly, depending on the outcome of the battle, which might start anytime in northern Kosovo, there could be some threat to our lives. If the convoy moves quickly, I think we might make it to the Macedonian border safely before the nationalist soldiers can catch up with us."

After a long pause, Servet abruptly asked, "Have you ever killed anyone?"

Jemal was surprised by this sudden question. He replied bashfully, "Yes, madam, two years ago during an infantry battle I killed an enemy soldier ... an unpleasant and painful memory."

Noticing Jemal's discomfort, Servet changed the subject. "Tell me about your wife. How old was she when your mother found her for you?"

Smiling broadly, Jemal replied, "My mother had nothing to do with my marriage. I eloped with Aisha when she was sixteen years old. She was from a neighboring village. To get married we ran away together to Sivas."

Raising her eyebrows, Servet asked, "Did she consent to being kidnapped?"

Controlling his urge to laugh, Jemal answered, "If she had not consented, I would have been killed later by her relatives. I met her for the first time at a wedding ceremony a year before we decided to run away. I was captivated by her beauty and wonderful smile. One late autumn afternoon, months later, I was able to meet her alone in the wheat fields before the harvest. We silently stared at each other for a long while, and then we talked and talked. A few days later, I met her again and asked her if she would marry me. She suddenly became very sad and informed me that her parents had promised to marry her to a relative. Without hesitation I told her that I would kidnap her. She smiled and replied that if we were caught, her relatives would kill us both. Then she whispered in my ear that she would like to spend the rest of her life with me. Then and there, we decided on the date of our great escape. One month later, on a Friday morning, we ran away to Sivas. The same day, a hodja married us. Afterward, we hid in my nephew's house in Sivas until both families agreed to accept our marriage and welcome us back to our respective villages."

Bedia suddenly began to cry. Servet clambered up into the cart. Before closing the canvas curtain behind her, she said, "You and Aisha chose each other without any undue impositions. You are lucky to have discovered one another in such a unique way."

Jemal pulled hard on the reins of the mule to join the quick-moving column of carts and supply wagons. The convoy was surrounded by a few soldiers on foot and horseback. After several hours of strenuous travel, the convoy suddenly came to a halt. During the next half hour, the horses, mules, and soldiers rested.

Soon after the convoy started moving again, Servet's cart passed a group of soldiers digging a large grave at the side of the road for patients who had died during the night. Jemal told Servet to look out through the canvas slit. Servet and Jemal, as they looked at the sad scene, prayed for the souls of the departed soldiers. Completing his prayers, Jemal spoke loudly to Servet, "Many more will die before we reach Skopje."

Over the next several long and arduous hours, the convoy lumbered until twilight at a slow but steady pace toward Macedonia.

Visiting the Gypsy Camp

Burhan was about to lead a couple of horses out of the stable when Michailovitch, struggling into his coat, ran toward him, shouting, "We are late! Let's go, Burhan!"

They rode west toward the Gypsy campground. For a while, they traveled side by side in silence. Eventually, Michailovitch began telling Burhan a bit of his life story.

"I was born about thirty years ago during the last great flood in a small town outside Belgrade. My mother told me that I was born on a boat while everything else in the town was under water. How about you? Where were you born?"

Burhan responded with the usual fictitious story of his origins. "I was born in Montenegro," he replied. "I was orphaned at a young age when my parents expired from consumption. Some relatives took care of me." To change the uneasy subject of his personal background, he then asked Michailovitch, "Why are we going to the Gypsy campground?"

Michailovitch nervously answered Burhan's question. "Today, we'll meet with an informer who'll identify a set of Turkish settlements in northern Kosovo that have not yet been evacuated. Tomorrow, we'll conduct raids on those settlements. Our commander has also asked me to do something special for him. We must take a few good-looking ladies to our camp to entertain the commander tonight."

Burhan, angered by such a petty assignment, attempted to disguise his true feelings with a pretentious laugh. "There are plenty of female prisoners in the camp, Lieutenant," he said nonchalantly. "Why don't you choose a few of them for the commander's pleasure?"

Grinning widely, Michailovitch answered, "Because the commander does not prefer Muslim women. We have to bring in a few Gypsy ladies. He thinks Muslim women will bring bad luck if he touches them. So we just have to find him a few good-looking Gypsy women, preferably young and fleshy. That's what he likes. In the meantime, let's hurry up and get to the Gypsy camp so we'll have time to enjoy ourselves."

When they arrived at the Gypsy camp, Burhan and Michailovitch were asked to join a group of Gypsies around a bonfire to share the morning meal. The informer, whose name was Goran, sat next to the lieutenant and talked nonstop for a long time. As he spoke, Goran pointed to a group of young women sitting at the fringe of the bonfire. He then asked Burhan and the lieutenant to follow him.

After a few minutes of chatting with the women, Michailovitch selected three and told Goran to get them ready for travel. He then requested that Goran send two of the youngest girls in the group to the trailers for the day's entertainment. Turning toward Burhan and laughing loudly, he told him it was his treat. "Go and enjoy yourself for a while," he said. "But remember, in a couple of hours we must leave for headquarters."

As he opened the door to the trailer, Goran wished Burhan a good time with the young lady. He told Burhan that he would knock on the door in two hours.

The inside of the trailer was warm, heavily perfumed and gaudy. In the far corner, a petite brunette Gypsy girl dressed in a colorful flared skirt and an elegant long-sleeved blouse was sitting at the edge of a small bed. She welcomed Burhan with a smile and asked him whether he would like a glass of wine.

As he sipped his wine, Burhan sat next to the small dining table. He asked the young girl her name, age, and where she was from.

As if she had not heard his questions, the girl kept silent as she started to slowly undress. Turning her back to Burhan to remove her blouse, she answered, "My name's Margarita, but my friends call me Rita. I'm seventeen years old. My upper half is Serbian and my lower half is a fun-loving Gypsy." After removing the last piece of clothing from her now completely naked body, she slowly walked toward Burhan. "You're a very handsome man," she said cheerfully. "What's your name? How old are you? Where do you come from?"

Grinning widely Burhan replied, "My name is Joseph. You can call me Joe. I'm old enough to come from the killing grounds."

As she stood next to him, Burhan noticed how attractive she was. She had long, shiny black hair gently rolling over her round shoulders, a handsome slender face with smooth skin, large dark eyes, long eyelashes, and well-trimmed eyebrows. Youthful energy flowed exuberantly from a well-shaped body with full hips, slender legs, and firm breasts.

She slowly reached out and stroked his hair. Burhan was aroused, but raised his hands to stop her. As she touched his lips with her fingertips, she asked, "What's wrong, Commander?"

Burhan closed his eyes to recall the times that he had made love to Katya. Since her tragic death more than two years earlier, he had felt no desire for sexual intercourse. Yet, at this moment, in front of this attractive young woman, his erotic instincts overcame his resistance. He reached out with both hands and slowly touched Rita's firm breasts and hardened nipples. He then gently moved his hands downward to her navel. Gently holding her waist with his left hand, he moved his right hand very slowly toward her pubic mound. He searched for, and finally felt on his fingertip, the moist entry to her vagina.

Trembling with excitement, he mumbled, "This is a place I haven't visited for a long time."

She stared into his dark green eyes and reached out and touched his light brown hair. She then leaned forward, kissed him on his forehead, and started to undress him. After she removed his underwear, she reached for his penis. She felt its gradual enlargement in her hands. Suddenly, she stopped and asked, "Are you a Muslim?"

After kissing her earlobe, Burhan whispered, "My upper half is a Montenegrin, and my lower half is a fun-loving Jew."

Back to Mitrovica

A few hours later, Michailovitch diligently studied the Gypsy women in the wagon. He commented on how pretty and charming they were, then abruptly turned toward Burhan and asked, "Should I start calling you Joe?"

Burhan, as he was getting on his horse, responded, "To the Gypsy lady, I'm just a Joe. For you, Lieutenant, I'll always be Burhan." Changing the subject, Burhan continued, "Could you tell me what type of information you received from Goran this morning?"

"I received exactly what I needed from him. His Gypsy friends living on the Ottoman side of the border have identified three small Turkish-Albanian towns for us to destroy. Tomorrow, we will attack the one with the weakest defenses, but first we must convince Commander Karaevitch to agree. Before that, the commander needs to have some fun. Later in the evening, we'll get his approval for the attack."

Over an hour later, as they reached the Sitnica River's bend toward the outskirts of Mitrovica, Michailovitch, putting his watch into his pocket, commented, "Today's adventure was about gathering information and having fun. Tomorrow, we'll have a bloody adventure destroying a few enemy towns."

Burhan did not respond. For him, attacking innocent civilians was not an honorable adventure but a savage and barbaric activity. As they rode into Mitrovica, Burhan pretended to listen to the lieutenant. He ignored Michailovitch's crude comments about the Turks and the Muslims; Burhan's mind was preoccupied with what Rita had told him earlier. During their steamy intercourse, she had mentioned that she was about to lose some very generous customers.

Recently, a senior Austrian officer had informed her that all the volunteers would soon be withdrawn to Vienna. This information had indicated a major change in the overall strategy of the Austro-Hungarian government.

Burhan turned toward Michailovitch. "Lieutenant," he said, "the young Gypsy woman told me that the Viennese volunteers are going back home."

After a loud gurgle, Michailovitch spat on the ground.

"Damn the Viennese! We don't need them."

Lieutenant Avni Rushes to Pristina

Lieutenant Avni tried his best to reach Pristina before noon. Yagiz galloped with all his strength toward the army command center. As he pushed the stallion to run faster, Avni thought about how surprised Mehmetali had been this morning when he had told him that they must report Burhan's information to the army intelligence. After Avni's warning, Mehmetali, deducing in his mind that both he and his son might be arrested, had insisted that he accompany Avni to Pristina. Ignoring the suggestion, Avni ordered Mehmetali to remain at camp.

Avni arrived at the army command center a few minutes before noon. He handed Yagiz over to a soldier at the main gate and rushed into the old two-story brick building. He was stopped by a military guard who asked Avni where he was going. Avni told the guard that he wanted to see the senior intelligence officer. The guard walked him into a cold, practically empty room, and asked him to take a seat and wait. Avni sat down on one of two chairs next to a small, dusty desk.

Almost half an hour later, a short, stocky captain entered the room. After greeting Avni, he asked, "How may I help you, Lieutenant?"

Slowly and in a low voice, Avni told the captain everything he had heard from Mehmetali, in detail. During the interview, Avni emphasized that Mehmetali had been a trusted recruit for a long time, and that he had lost one of his sons in one of the recent southern Serbia defense battles. "Unfortunately," Avni said, "his other son joined the nationalist forces last year. They did not see each other until very recently."

Avni then explained to the captain that the recent encounter between father and son had happened solely by chance, because his son had been on an intelligence mission arranged by the nationalist army command to assess the Ottoman troop locations and their artillery strength. "When they met," Avni emphasized, "Mehmetali's son informed his father that the nationalist army had received considerable military equipment from the European powers and thousands of new volunteers from the Austro-Hungarian Empire. The presence of a large number of well-trained voluntary conscripts from Vienna poses a serious threat to our army."

When the captain questioned the validity of the information, Avni responded, "I guarantee that Mehmetali is telling the truth, but I'm not so sure about his son. If Burhan is telling the truth, we're definitely facing a formidable enemy. In that case, it may be better to withdraw to Macedonia. But if Burhan is giving us misinformation, withdrawal will be a drastic mistake."

The captain abruptly interrupted Avni and suggested that he not second-guess his commanding officers. He then ordered Avni to wait in the room until the matter had been discussed with the head of the intelligence unit. Then the captain stood up, turned on his heel, and left the room.

He returned an hour later just as Avni was about to finish a bowl of hot Turkish lentil soup. The captain sat down and remained silent allowing Avni to finish his meal. Then he spoke. "Lieutenant, it is the decision of our commander that you return to your unit immediately and follow your original orders. You will be accompanied by a military guard who will bring Mehmetali here to the army headquarters for questioning. After questioning, he must be isolated in a cell to prevent any more information or misinformation from being channeled through him. If what you say about him is true, he will not be punished. No harm will come to him in the isolation cell. If we decide to withdraw, he will also be evacuated to Skopje."

Both officers rose and saluted each other. The captain thanked Lieutenant Avni for his courage and honesty in bringing this information to the attention of the army intelligence unit.

Late in the afternoon, Avni, accompanied by a military guard, returned to the Yanyevo regiment's camp and immediately summoned Mehmetali. Avni informed him that the following morning he would be taken to the military intelligence unit for questioning. He would then be placed in an isolation cell until the end of the upcoming battle. He assured Mehmetali that under no circumstances would he be punished.

Turning pale, Mehmetali mumbled, "I'm not afraid of dying, but I don't want to be tortured."

Understanding his friend's fear, Avni replied, "If the intelligence officers were suspicious of the truth of this matter, I would have been arrested immediately. You would also have been thrown in jail. Now all they want is for you to tell them directly what you know. They want to keep you isolated because they don't want Burhan contacting you again. Trust me, my old friend. You'll be in a safer place during the upcoming battle. You'll stay alive."

Mehmetali, smiling meekly, responded, "That's if they don't kill me first." He walked up to Avni and gave him a gentle hug. "I may not see you again," he mumbled. "Lieutenant Avni, I want you to know that you are like a son to me. I'll keep you in my prayers so that you'll survive and be with your family again. God bless you!"

Avni sadly watched the military guard escort his dear old comrade-in-arms through the massive campground.

Turkish Villagers Join the Convoy

Immediately before sunset, Lieutenant Nihad, on horseback, approached Servet's slowly moving cart. He asked Jemal if everything was all right.

"Everything is fine, Lieutenant," replied Jemal.

Hearing voices, Servet opened the canvas cover and asked the lieutenant what was slowing them down. Lieutenant Nihad explained that the weather conditions and the burial of casualties were the main reasons for the occasional halts.

After abruptly ordering Jemal to be on guard for snipers, Nihad said, "You are also expected to stand for a couple of hours of night guard duty. Report to the security sergeant of your column at exactly twenty hundred hours."

Lieutenant Nihad, noticing that Servet was no longer watching, told Jemal to come closer.

"This morning we received a message from Colonel Husnu. The Pristina headquarters reported that several small bands of Serbian nationalist soldiers and Albanian irregulars might be planning to attack Yanyevo, and possibly the evacuation convoy. Please, keep this information to yourself, and if an unexpected attack does occur, be prepared to defend the family you are responsible for. Yesterday, a large group of Turkish villagers from Pristina, mostly old men, women, and children, joined our convoy. The leader of the villagers reported to me that a small band of Albanian insurgents attacked them two days ago. The villagers were able to defend themselves, but lost seventeen lives. This group of villagers included a few feisty old men with a fighting spirit." Pointing at the end of the convoy, the lieutenant continued, "They're following the convoy. They will provide us with some rear-guard protection."

Returning Jemal's salute, Nihad turned his horse around and galloped toward the head of the convoy. An hour later, the weather suddenly turned stormy. A heavy snowfall stalled the convoy for many hours.

After ensuring that Servet and the baby were comfortable under the protective canvas of the cart, Jemal walked to the tail end of the convoy to speak with the migrating Turkish villagers. Arriving at the now-extended end of the convoy, he was greeted by a tall, muscular old man named Selim. Meeting Jemal, Selim offered him a rolled tobacco leaf to smoke. He explained that he was the leader of a village south of Pristina. Sitting under a makeshift tent on the side of a wagon full of children, Selim and Jemal talked for a long time, smoking tobacco and sipping hot tea. When one of the villagers asked if Jemal had any children, he answered, "Yes, I have a son called Selim." Looking at the village head, he continued, "The same name as yours."

Jemal later returned to the cart laden with food and hot tea for Servet. The Turkish villagers had insisted that Servet must be properly nourished to care for her infant.

The Twelfth of January: Mehmetali in Jail

During the late afternoon, as he checked the battle preparations of the Yanyevo unit, Lieutenant Avni decided to send the young soldier Avni to Pristina to determine the whereabouts of Mehmetali. He had been taken to the headquarters by the military guard in the very early hours of the morning. After completing his routine investigation, Avni summoned the young soldier to his tent and ordered him to go immediately with the supply sergeant to Pristina.

"While the sergeant is getting the necessary food supplies, you find out where Mehmetali is. He's possibly being kept in an isolation room in the main operations building, next to the command center." Handing the young soldier a few Ottoman coins, Avni continued, "If the guards don't allow you to visit Mehmetali, give them the coins so they will let you see him. Return tomorrow afternoon with the supply unit. Dismissed!"

After the departure of the young soldier, a messenger from Pristina headquarters hurriedly entered Avni's tent. He gave the lieutenant an envelope from the Yanyevo hospital. Dismissing the messenger, Avni opened the envelope from Colonel Husnu. The message was short and concise. It said that the evacuation convoy had left Yanyevo and was traveling slowly but safely toward Skopje, expected to arrive within four days. The news put Avni's mind at rest. *Thank God,* he thought. *In a few days Servet and Bedia will be in a safer place.*

He sat on his cot and put the note from Colonel Husnu into his mailbag. Realizing that he had not yet received any specific orders from the army command center detailing changes in the battle plan, he concluded that his intelligence report had not been believed. Yet, regardless of the command center's apparent mistrust, Avni was now fully convinced that Mehmetali's information had been an accurate description of the actual military situation in Kosovo. According to the latest instructions he had received, in two days' time the Ottoman army would conduct a counteroffensive at the northwest end of Kosovo Polje with the intent of pushing the enemy back to southern Serbia. The standing order for his unit was to protect the artillery positions on the northeastern hills of Kosovo. During the next two days, he was ordered to move his troops into the foothills to protect the artillery units from enemy attacks.

Avni, thinking and rethinking the strategic importance of the assignment given to his unit, concluded that the Yanyevo unit's untrained local recruits and the exhausted regular soldiers would not be able to defend the artillery positions if a full enemy charge took place. *Since we are engaging in a counteroffensive strategy,* he speculated, *the best the Yanyevo troops could accomplish would be to prevent infiltration by destroying the scouts sent to determine the locations of the Ottoman artillery positions spread over the hills.*

Hearing the supper gong, Avni left the tent to join his soldiers for the evening meal. Given the fact that his small unit had been charged with defending a considerably large area, Lieutenant Avni wanted a general discussion with his section commanders. He asked all the troop leaders to sit close to him at the table. They then discussed in detail how best to prevent the advancing enemy troops from reaching the artillery positions.

A Sick Child

Because of frequent stops en route to Skopje, the evacuation convoy made slow progress toward its final destination. Just before sunset, the convoy stopped for the night. After Jemal had built a fire, Servet descended from the cart and asked Jemal to fetch one of the nurses attending the patients. Jemal asked if she was sick. Servet answered that Bedia was ill with diarrhea and high fever.

Selim, the headman of the migrating Turkish villagers, greeted both Servet and Jemal as he passed by the cart. Noticing that Jemal was about to leave, he hollered, "Young man, where are you rushing off to? The food rations will not be ready for another hour."

Jemal explained that Servet Hanim's baby girl was sick. "I've got to go look for a nurse," he replied loudly.

Selim, without hesitation, asked Jemal to stay with Servet and make sure they were comfortable. "Jemal," he said, "I'll fetch the nurse."

More than half an hour later, Selim returned, not with a nurse, but with several Turkish village women. He explained that the nurses were busy caring for the wounded soldiers. Selim told Servet that one of the nurses might be able to stop by later to examine the baby.

"Servet Hanim, you don't need to worry," Selim said. "My wife and her friends would like to help you with your sick child. We have some good traditional remedies to help your little one recover quickly."

During the next several hours, the village women took good care of little Bedia. They fed her some powerful concoctions that helped her recover quickly. Their attention to Bedia allowed the exhausted mother some time to rest. When Jemal returned from guard duty, Selim and his wife were still with Servet and Bedia. Shortly afterward, as they were about to leave, Jemal thanked them profusely and wished them a safe evening and a good night's rest.

The Thirteenth of January: A Deadly Attack

The next morning before sunrise, Jemal was startled by the sound of nearby gunshots. He bolted from the tent with rifle in hand and ran toward the cart. Holding Bedia in her arms tightly, Servet was struggling to climb down the cart. "What's going on Jemal?" she asked. "Are we being attacked? What should we do?"

Jemal told her to be calm, took the baby from her and helped Servet descend. While Servet hurriedly wrapped Bedia with several blankets, Jemal quickly put together a well-covered hiding place close to the ground and under the cart, hopefully safe from stray bullets. Jemal helped mother and child hide under the cart, and draped them with blankets for additional protection. As he turned around, Jemal saw several men on horses galloping away. The uniforms they wore indicated that they were irregular Serbian nationalist soldiers. As they galloped, they occasionally turned around to fire on the convoy. As Jemal raised his rifle and aimed at the enemy, several

Ottoman soldiers on horseback passed him by. As they chased after the enemy, one of the soldiers shouted at Jemal not to shoot. Putting his rifle aside, Jemal knelt next to the cart, assuring Servet that it was now safe to come out.

Jemal helped Servet climb up into the cart. As he was handing Bedia to her mother, Jemal noticed several medics running toward the end of the convoy. He realized that the attack had taken place near the tail end of the convoy, where the Turkish villagers had camped for the night. He told Servet he was going to check on Selim and his entourage. He then ran toward the end of the convoy.

By the time Jemal arrived at the Turkish villagers' camp, soldiers were everywhere. He saw several wounded villagers on the snow-covered ground. It was clear that several old men, women, and children had been shot while trying to hide. A few of the wounded were being attended to by medics. Others, lying motionless on the ground, were not getting any attention -- either because they were already dead or too badly wounded to survive. Jemal saw Selim at the far end of the camp. A medic was on his knees helping a wounded person, with Selim standing by his side. As he approached the old man, Jemal noticed that the victim was Selim's wife; she lay on the ground in a pool of blood. The medic was trying desperately to stop the bleeding.

Selim, groaning, went down on his knees and held his wife's hand. He repeated his wife's name and kept calling on the Lord to help her.

The medic finally stopped working on the patient. Turning toward Selim, he said, "Father, your wife is no longer with us. May her soul rest in peace."

Selim wiped his tears with a large linen handkerchief. As the old man cried and prayed, Jemal offered what little comfort he could. The medic left them alone and moved on to help the other wounded.

"We were together for fifty years," Selim whispered. "We raised six children: three boys and three girls. Several years ago, two of our sons died fighting on the eastern front. One of my daughters, who lived in a village in southern Serbia, died a few months ago at the hands of Serbian nationalists. My youngest daughter was shot dead during an attack on our group two days before we joined your convoy. Now, I've lost my wife, the mother of my children. I don't know if any of us will survive to see peace."

After a long moment of silence, Selim selflessly asked how the baby was. Jemal reported that, thanks to the efforts of his wife the previous night, the baby had recovered quickly.

Selim gracefully covered his wife's body and face with a white linen sheet and got to his feet. "Jemal, would you please help me count the dead and wounded?"

As they tried to determine the number of casualties, they walked around and consoled all the surviving villagers.

Completing the count, Selim proclaimed, "Seven dead and eight wounded, three of whom are not expected to survive. How many more days do we have to travel before we reach Skopje?"

Jemal reluctantly replied, "We have two more travel days ahead of us, Selim *Baba*."

A few minutes later, Lieutenant Nihad joined them. He sincerely expressed his condolences to Selim for the loss of his wife, and then asked grieving man to describe in detail what had happened early that morning.

Selim calmly began explaining. "Lieutenant, just before sunrise, as some of the men and I were about to complete our morning prayers, we were attacked by several nationalist bastards. Before we could retrieve our guns to return fire, they had shot at anything that moved. Many women and children panicked and ran through the campground. Everyone was scrambling to find a place to hide, as if they were being chased by wild animals. We managed to shoot and kill two of them. We lost two elderly men, two women, and three children. Of the eight wounded, only five are expected to survive."

Lieutenant Nihad ordered the soldiers to build a fire and prepare food and tea for the survivors. Jemal asked the lieutenant if Servet Hanim could join them around the fire. Tradition did not usually allow men and women to mingle, but since many village women were tending to wounded men, the lieutenant agreed.

Jemal raced to the cart, where he found Servet trying to start a fire. He told her about the horrible incidents in detail. Servet, hearing of the death of Selim's wife, began to cry. When Jemal informed her that the lieutenant had asked her to join everyone around the big fire in the villagers' camp, wiping her tears, she responded, "Little Bedia is asleep, so I must decline the lieutenant's invitation."

"Madam, I'll ask one of the young girls from the village camp to stay with the baby," Jemal replied. "Please, come to the camp once she arrives."

"That'll be fine, Jemal. I would like to see Selim Baba to give him my condolences." Handing a couple of empty hot-water bottles to Jemal, she continued, "Please, ask the young girl to fill these bottles with hot water and bring them to me. I must keep the cart warm for Bedia."

"Certainly, madam; I'll get them filled for you."

A few minutes later a young village girl dressed in a colorful vest and *shalvar* arrived. With a smile, she handed the hot-water bottles to Servet. After positioning the bottles next to the sleeping baby, Servet snuggled Bedia into a warm cocoon of blankets. She then walked briskly toward the tail end of the convoy.

After passing dozens of wagons and carts, Servet came upon a very disturbing scene. Ahead she saw a dead horse and the blood-soaked bodies of two enemy soldiers on the ground. A short distance later, she came upon the bodies of four slain elderly men and women, one of whom was Selim's wife. Then she noticed three dead children sprawled on the blood-soaked snow. With tears in her eyes, she knelt to pray for the dead. After completing her prayers, she cursed the enemy for killing innocent women and children. She got to her feet, turned around, and looked at the big bonfire a few meters ahead. Many people were gathered around the fire: the wounded covered with blankets and surrounded by village women and medics, the old village men leaning on their rifles, and soldiers excitedly talking to each other. Servet recognized Selim sitting among the village men and moved toward him to express her condolences. She gently touched his shoulder. The old man, turning around, rose to his feet at once.

With tears in her eyes, Servet said, "Selim Baba, may God grant your wife eternal peace, and give you the patience and strength to live the rest of your life in good health."

Standing next to the old man, Lieutenant Nihad respectfully invited Servet to join them. Jemal brought her an army stool and placed it close to the fire. Appreciating the warmth, she thanked the lieutenant for inviting her. "Lieutenant Nihad," Servet asked, "have you received any news from the front?"

"Yes, madam. I have received the news that fighting has not started yet. Today or tomorrow a broad enemy attack is expected. As indicated by today's attack, some of the irregular enemy units have penetrated the Ottoman defense lines. In addition to our convoy, many southern Kosovo settlements have been attacked over the past two days. I fear they may attack our convoy again. For everyone's safety, we must travel faster toward Skopje."

Lieutenant Nihad then ordered several soldiers, including Jemal, to help the villagers bury the dead. He ordered the sergeant to prepare the convoy to move within the hour. After once again expressing his condolences to Selim, Lieutenant Nihad offered to walk Servet back to her cart.

On the way, Servet asked the young lieutenant, "I don't understand why the enemy is so aggressive and vicious. Don't they know we are retreating?"

"Yes, they know we're retreating to Macedonia," replied Nihad. "But our retreat does not end their struggle to establish a greater Serbia. They hope this will also include Macedonia. Their strategy of frightening the Muslim population of Kosovo and southern Serbia away from the territory is part of a greater game. This morning's attack on our convoy was a ploy to scare and demoralize our troops in Kosovo and Macedonia. When we reach Skopje tomorrow, God willing, everyone in our convoy will tell others in the city about these vicious attacks. Rumors that the conflict has now reached the borders of Macedonia will cause general panic throughout the Muslim population."

Straightening the scarf covering her hair, Servet responded, "What you say makes sense, but where does it all end?"

Nihad stopped walking and turned toward Servet. "Madam," he said smartly. "It would be impossible for me to guess where and when this onslaught on our empire will end. In addition to the conflicts in the Balkans, we may face serious military threats on the eastern front and in some of our North African provinces. Yet, the Balkan conflict is significant primarily because it is so close to the seat of the Ottoman government. A collaborative military effort by the Serbians, the Greeks, and the Bulgarians could be a serious military threat to us. I fear that this conflict in Serbia is just the beginning of our final struggle to keep our foothold in Europe. What's most threatening is that the Turkish, Albanian, and Slavic Muslim populations of the Balkans have been slowly pushed from their lands during the conflicts of the past decade. The essence of these struggles in the Balkans now appears to be the result of rising nationalism as much as the clash of religions. This process of depopulating the Balkans of Muslims almost guarantees a final victory to the Christian ethnic groups. But then, I wonder how all these Christian minorities with different ethnic persuasions will be able to coexist with each other. For example, Servet Hanim, in Macedonia the Turks, Albanians, and Macedonian Muslims have lived in harmony for centuries. In addition, Macedonian Christians, Serbs, Greeks, Bulgarians, Armenians, Jews, and Gypsies have coexisted in this wonderful land. If we lose the coming battles in old Serbia and Kosovo, we'll soon face new battles that will reach into Macedonia and the western Thrace."

Lieutenant Nihad completed his succinct historical and military analysis and abruptly bid Servet farewell. He ordered the soldier following them to bring his horse. As he mounted his horse, he pointedly added, "Servet Hanim, I hope the good Lord will protect your husband during the coming battles so that he can meet his little girl."

Servet, appreciating his words of good-will, thanked the young lieutenant, and rushed into the cart to check on little Bedia.

The Interrogation of Mehmetali

Two well-armed military guards accompanied Mehmetali to the main operations building next to the command center. As the rusty, old iron door swung shut behind them, the guards jokingly told Mehmetali that the evening feast would be served after sunset. Once his vision had adjusted to the darkness of the cold isolation cell, Mehmetali tried to pull himself together. During the past several hours, he had been interrogated by several different groups of officers. They kept asking the same questions over and over. He had told them exactly what he had told Lieutenant Avni three days earlier. The last officer that had interrogated Mehmetali had informed him that tomorrow would bring yet more questions.

Exhausted, Mehmetali lay on the wooden bunk bed and fell into a deep sleep within minutes.

Many hours later, the noise of a key unlocking the door to his cell awakened him. The heavy iron door opened with a screech, and a young Ottoman soldier entered the dark cell, balancing a large tin plate in one hand and a candle in the other.

Mehmetali, throwing both legs over the side of his bed, sat on the edge of the bunk. "What do you want?" he gruffly asked.

The young soldier, handing over the tin plate heaped with food, replied, "Greetings, Uncle Mehmetali!"

Still feeling drowsy, Mehmetali tried to shake off the grogginess of his interrupted sleep. He struggled to see the young soldier's face through the shimmering candle light. The voice was definitely familiar. He gradually recognized the youthful face of Avni, the young recruit from Yanyevo. He rose to his feet and warmly embraced the young soldier.

"Son, what are you doing here?"

"Lieutenant Avni ordered me to come to Pristina to find you. He gave me some money to pay the guards to take good care of you. After I paid them, I became their good friend, and they allowed me to bring this meal to you."

"That's very nice of the lieutenant," said Mehmetali. "When are you going back to the camp?"

"I was supposed to go back to the camp with the supply team today, but I didn't want to leave without seeing you. I sent a message to the lieutenant that I would return early tomorrow morning. He expects a report from me about your health and whereabouts. So tell me, how did the intelligence officers treat you?"

Mehmetali, appreciating the genuine concern and care extended by the lieutenant and the young soldier, told him that he had been treated well. He asked young Avni to tell the lieutenant not to worry about him.

The Fourteenth of January: Back to Jail

The next morning, immediately after the morning prayers, Mehmetali was removed from his cell by guards and taken to the interrogation room for more of the same treatment he had received the day before. As he waited in the cold and empty room, he looked out the window and watched the soft wind blow snow from the pine trees in the courtyard below. He felt the welcoming but eerie calmness that usually precedes a disaster. He had a premonition that something bad was about to happen. As the door creaked open, he turned around to greet the Ottoman officer, who took the seat behind the desk and gazed sternly at him.

After a long pause, the officer told Mehmetali that there would be no more questions. "The information that you have given us has been confirmed," the officer said grimly. "You will be returned to the isolation cell until orders for your release are received." The officer arose, opened the door, and ordered the guard outside to take Mehmetali back to the isolation cell. Noting the confusion on Mehmetali's face, the officer softly said, "Don't worry! You'll be all right. This is for your own safety."

After Mehmetali had departed for his cell, the intelligence officer immediately went to his supervisor's office. Sharply saluting, he asked, "Captain, when are we meeting with the general staff to discuss the implementation of this morning's decision? Aren't we required to inform all regiments and units that we are now withdrawing to southern Kosovo?"

The captain, hurriedly stuffing some documents into a leather pouch, turned around and replied, "That is a very smart idea, Lieutenant! Immediately assemble all senior staff for a meeting."

Serbians in Kosovo

Burhan awoke much earlier than usual. He quietly got dressed and left the crowded sleeping quarters for some fresh air. Pulling the chilly morning air deep into his lungs, he gazed up at the sky. He could still see the stars, an indication that a cold, clear, and sunny day lay ahead. He walked to the mess hall for breakfast. After taking a couple of freshly baked rolls and a cup of tea from the kitchen counter, he sat at a large wooden table to eat.

Alone in the huge mess hall, Burhan wondered about the day's prospects. He had not seen Michailovitch since they returned from the Gypsy camp a day earlier. Hearing the hinges of the big wooden door squeak, he silently resented this intrusion into his cherished morning solitude. Unexpectedly, he heard Lieutenant Michailovitch calling to the soldier on duty to bring some dried goat cheese to go with his bread.

Cradling the cup of hot tea in his hands, Burhan turned toward the kitchen counter. "Good morning, Lieutenant!" he shouted.

With a plate of bread and cheese, Michailovitch joined Burhan for breakfast. Noticing that Burhan had no cheese with his bread, a privilege bestowed only on officers, he handed him a large piece. "Burhan," Michailovitch began gleefully. "Yesterday evening's entertainment was a great success. The commander had a great time and loved the ladies we brought for him. By the way, before he got completely drunk, he agreed with my proposal that we conduct preliminary attacks on some key towns and villages in Kosovo before the main assault. During the unit commanders' meeting last night, we had to decide which unit should attack which town. I volunteered our unit for an attack on the two large, mostly defenseless villages at the southwest end of the Ottoman lines. I think it was in one of these villages that you began your secret fact-finding mission last week. Since you know the area well, it will be easier for us to conduct effective assaults on these villages, with minimal losses."

Recalling his earlier discussion with the commander, Burhan commented, "Lieutenant, the commander promised me that the family of Ismet the collaborator would be protected."

"I don't know what you're talking about," snapped Michailovitch. "Anyway, who cares about a dead collaborator's Albanian family? We have to get rid of all Muslims -- Turks or Albanians. We will go into those villages, cause the greatest damage in the shortest possible time, and get the hell out. Don't forget we have to destroy two villages in the next two days. We don't have the time to be selective. We'll soon depart with fifty well-armed men. Now, go help with the preparations. I will meet the company in front of the armory in one hour. I expect them to be fully mounted and ready to move out."

It took Michailovitch and the company half a day to reach the area where the two Turkish-Albanian villages were located. While riding, Burhan kept thinking about Michailovitch's stance on sparing Ismet's family. He decided that, regardless of what Michailovitch had said, he would do whatever possible to protect them. Unfortunately, he had no specific plan for how to accomplish that. He knew well from past experience that surprise attacks precluded typical military conduct, and the principles that normally protect a civilian population were all pushed aside. Most of the men would be out of control and unleash all sorts of violence against the civilians.

When we attack the village, Burhan thought, *I should get close to Ismet's house and keep an eye on the soldiers.* He also kept thinking about the general attack that would begin soon. He doubted the rumor he had heard from the young Gypsy prostitute about the Viennese volunteers' withdrawal to Austria-Hungary. The nationalists would not proceed with their overall attack to liberate Kosovo without the Austrian volunteers. He believed his unit had become an essential part of the move to push the Ottomans further east, resulting in the liberation of Kosovo.

"This isn't liberation," he murmured. *This is trading one form of tyranny for another. The coming tyranny will be especially worse for us Albanians, for sure.*

The company dismounted at the forested area where Burhan had left Ismet barely a week earlier. As they had their lunch, the lieutenant assembled the troop leaders to discuss strategy. Michailovitch decided to launch the attack on the first Turkish-Albanian village late in the afternoon, just before sunset. Afterward, the troops could retreat to the forest for the night. The lieutenant then announced, "Early tomorrow morning, we will attack another village several kilometers southeast of this one. Then, depending on the circumstances, we will join other assault units for a concerted attack on Grachanitsa and Pristina, either later tomorrow or the following day."

Ottoman Withdrawal to Kumanovo

Avni was overwhelmed with conflicting emotions of anxiety and contentment. He had just received a special dispatch from regimental headquarters that all previous orders were to be disregarded. His unit was now ordered to provide peripheral protection to the infantry and cavalry forces during the staged withdrawal. The new orders he had received from headquarters indicated that most of the infantry, cavalry, and artillery units were to withdraw immediately to Kumanovo, a town near the Kosovo-Macedonia border. Once there, the Ottoman army would establish a new defensive line against the Serbian forces. Upon successful completion of the first stage of withdrawal to Kumanovo, the army units in Macedonia would be instructed to relocate north of Tetovo to establish a secondary line of defense. Heavy reinforcements from the Ottoman army's Thracian regiment were expected to arrive at Kumanovo to strengthen the overall defensive capacity of the new front. Avni was highly impressed with this timely decision to withdraw and establish a better defensive line to prevent the enemy's possible advance into Macedonia. Combining Macedonian and Thracian army regiments had probably become possible through recent diplomatic agreements with the Bulgarians, whereby some of the Thracian army units could be sent to Macedonia and Kosovo to reinforce the new front line.

Avni wondered how the Serbian nationalist army would react to this new situation. If he were in their place, he would attack in an effort to cause the greatest damage to the withdrawing Ottoman army. Obviously, this possibility had already been considered by the Ottoman military intelligence. A considerable number of army units, including infantry, cavalry, and light artillery, would stage a mock offensive action from the area north of Kosovo Polje, the Field of Blackbirds, toward the nationalist army concentrations southeast of Mitrovica.

The Yanyevo unit was now ordered to cover the right flank of the mock offensive, and to provide infantry protection to the heavy artillery units withdrawing to Kumanovo. The Ottoman Army's general command hoped that the planned mock offensive would keep the main forces of the Serbian nationalist army preoccupied for at least a day or two, allowing the withdrawing Ottoman forces time to regroup. Survivors of the mock assault were to withdraw under cover of darkness and move toward southern Kosovo.

Laying down the new orders, Avni ordered the staff sergeant to inform the troop leaders to join him. Before leaving the tent, the staff sergeant informed the lieutenant that the young soldier Avni was waiting outside the tent to see him.

When young Avni entered the tent, the lieutenant ordered him to report on his mission to Pristina.

Standing erect in the middle of the tent, the young soldier bellowed, "Lieutenant, as ordered, I located Mehmetali. I met him last night. You were right. He was locked up in an isolation cell in the main operations building. He seemed well, and told me that he was being treated with respect."

Lieutenant Avni thanked the young soldier, and, before dismissing him, ordered him to report his arrival to the guard-duty sergeant. After the soldier's departure, Avni walked out of the tent and approached the troop leaders, who were anxiously awaiting their commanding officer.

A Village Marked for Destruction

Toward the end of the rainy, cold afternoon, fifty well-armed members of the nationalist special attack unit entered the outskirts of Ismet's village. The unit's commander, Lieutenant Michailovitch, selected two groups of ten men to attack the local police office and the gendarme station, which were near each other. He told the other soldiers to spread out in groups of three and attack local residences. He ordered that all males, regardless of age, be killed.

As a leering grin distorted his face, he commanded, "Do not take any action against residents until attacks on the police and the gendarmes have begun. Give us a fifteen-minute lead before you make your move. What you do with the females is entirely up to you. Take your pick for the night's entertainment."

Burhan kept a low profile and was not selected to be in the primary attack units. He wanted to stay behind to provide some protection to Ismet's family. As he prepared to lead the main attack group down the hilly road, Michailovitch turned to Burhan and ordered him to take charge of all the units that would attack residential areas. He instructed Burhan to ensure that all units inflicted maximum damage on the civilians and their properties.

"Remember, have no mercy!" Michailovitch shouted. "Eliminate them all! Take no prisoners, except a few women for tonight's entertainment. Burn the houses down. Leave the village before sunset and go to the area where we set up camp this morning."

Feeling blessed by this sudden stroke of good luck, Burhan saluted Michailovitch. With a mischievous grin, he replied, "Yes, Lieutenant. What needs to be done will be done."

He could now definitely provide some protection to Ismet's family. As the group leaders circled around him, he assigned them in small groups to various parts of the village except the area where Ismet's house was located. He saved that area for himself. He selected two men with some degree of intelligence and maturity to join him. After everyone had dispersed in various directions, Burhan and the two soldiers created mayhem in Ismet's neighborhood. They entered houses and shot at anything that moved.

As always, Burhan refrained from killing women and children and made sure that the two Serbian soldiers also refrained from shooting them. One exception to this rule occurred unexpectedly. As they entered a house one block up the hill from Ismet's residence, they were fired on by a young boy. The soldier next to Burhan took a bullet in his chest. The other Serbian soldier fired his gun at the young boy, killing him instantly. The soldier then entered the main room and chased after several screaming women and young children trying to escape through the window. Distraught by the loss of his comrade, he brutally fired upon them.

Storming into the room, Burhan grabbed the Serbian soldier by the shoulder and ordered him to stop. The soldier turned his gun on him and snarled, "You goddamn Muslim shit, don't ever touch me." Burhan, holding his revolver at hip level, fired immediately. The soldier hit the floor with a fatal wound to his abdomen.

Burhan, as he removed the rifle from the dying soldier's hand, peeked into the room. He saw bloody bodies of women and children tangled and motionless on the floor. He entered the room to check if anyone had survived. Suddenly, one of the motionless bodies on the floor leapt to her feet. Screaming and slashing with a long butcher knife, she viciously attacked Burhan. Quickly grabbing her wrist, Burhan struck her head with the butt of his revolver, knocking her back to the floor. She fell unconscious on the dead bodies of two children spread-eagled on the wooden floor.

Burhan sat next to her and tied her hands and feet. His attacker was a pretty, young girl, tall and strong in appearance. A few minutes later, as she slowly regained consciousness, she tried to spit in his face. Burhan shouted at her in Turkish to stop and behave. "That is, if you would like to stay alive," he said abruptly.

She did not answer; she turned her head away to hide her tears.

"I'm leaving now," Burhan said. "You must stay put. If you start screaming, soldiers will find you. If anyone comes into this room, pretend you're dead. I'll come back for you later."

Burhan got up, slung the rifle over his left shoulder and walked out of the house. He ran down the street toward Ismet's residence. He heard gunshots nearby and saw women and children running every which way. Within a few minutes he reached Ismet's house. He kicked the door open, entered the house and carefully checked every room. Suddenly, as he entered the kitchen, he came face-to-face with Dursun, who was pointing an old revolver ready to fire. After a short stare at Burhan's face, Dursun pulled the trigger and the gun's cock snapped into firing position. Fortunately for Burhan, the old gun failed to ignite.

Burhan raised his rifle, pointing it at Dursun's chest, and got ready to fire. Before he pulled the trigger, however, Burhan noticed Dursun's wife and his infant son in the corner of the room. Upon seeing them, he refrained from firing the gun.

Dursun had already recognized Burhan. Realizing that he was about to be killed, he cursed loudly. "You're a filthy traitor! Go ahead! Shoot me!"

Keeping his gun still pointed at Dursun, Burhan yelled back, "I didn't come here to harm you or anyone in your family."

He ordered Dursun to turn around and lie face down on the floor next to his family. He informed the family that the nationalist soldiers were here to destroy the village. He then asked Dursun where the rest of the family was.

"When we heard the gunshots," Dursun replied, "my great uncle and my aunt left the house with the younger women and children. They went to hide in the woods."

Burhan was perplexed. "Why didn't you go with them?" he asked.

After throwing a hefty spit on the floor, Dursun answered, "Remembering that you and Uncle Ismet disappeared into the woods, I felt it was not a smart thing to do. I told them not to go into the forest. But they wouldn't listen to me."

Burhan continued questioning Dursun. "Is there a cellar in this house?" After Dursun's affirmation, Burhan told him to hide in the cellar with his family and leave the house in the morning before sunrise.

"Go to Skopje to save yourself and your family," Burhan said. "Do not go through Pristina; go around the city by circling its southwestern periphery. Don't use the main roads. Travel toward Skopje through secluded, wooded areas."

Getting to his feet, Dursun limped to the middle of the kitchen. He pulled on the handle of a wooden hatch on the floor. After guiding his family into the cellar's wooden staircase, which led down to the storage area under the house, he stood on the stairway and turned around. "Why are you doing this?" he asked.

"Your Uncle Ismet gave his life to save mine. I'm paying off my debt," replied Burhan.

As he helped his family down the steep stairs, Dursun commented, "Do you know I almost killed my uncle that evening when you were here in this house?"

Burhan held the wooden hatch open for Dursun to descend. "Yes, your uncle told me. I'm going to ask you a favor, Dursun. There's a young Turkish girl four houses up the hill on the other side of the street. All her family members are dead. I'm going to bring her here in a short while. I'm sure you know her. Please, help her get away with you to Skopje."

"Yes, I know the house," said Dursun. "She must be one of the daughters of Hasan Efendi, the owner of the coffee shop in the village square. I'll help her to safety."

Before closing the cellar hatch, Burhan handed his revolver to Dursun. "Thank God, your antique gun didn't fire, otherwise I'd be dead. Use this one to protect your family. Good luck!" He closed the hatch, and placed an old kilim over it.

The street outside Ismet's house was now strangely quiet. Many dead bodies were strewn about the wide dirt road. Several houses in the street below were on fire. It appeared that nationalist soldiers were about to move into Ismet's neighborhood to burn the houses down. Burhan realized that he should get the young Turkish girl out of harm's way before the soldiers with torches reached the houses on Ismet's street. He rushed into the house where she had been left tied on the floor. In the hallway, he stopped to take the revolver from the dead Serbian soldier and put it in his holster. He stepped into the room to find the young girl. She was sitting on the floor, looking at him with wide eyes full of fear.

Burhan sat on the floor next to her. "Young lady," he said, "what's your name?"

Without looking at him, she answered, "Nurjahan!"

"Listen to me very carefully, Nurjahan. I'll take you to another house where an Albanian family is hiding in the cellar. The Albanian man's name is Dursun. You just follow him to safety. Please remember, when we're out on the street, you must behave. Don't do anything crazy, just be calm and control yourself. When you see the Serbian soldiers, don't panic, don't look at them, keep your head down, and follow my instructions."

Burhan walked out of the house with the young Turkish girl whose hands still were loosely tied behind her back. She followed Burhan closely. Suddenly, two nationalist soldiers ran toward Burhan. One stopped in front of him to stare at the pretty young girl. With a sneer on his face, he hollered, "Sergeant, you've discovered a treasure for the night!"

The other soldier, torch in hand, first saluted and then reported, "The lieutenant is looking for you, Sergeant."

Burhan quickly turned toward the soldier who had made the crude comment earlier and ordered him to throw the torch in his hand onto the ground. He then asked the other soldier, "Where's the lieutenant?"

"He is with several women prisoners in a house a few blocks down the street. I think he's selecting a few female companions for the night."

Pulling the young girl along by her arm, Burhan ordered both soldiers to stop burning houses and gather everyone at the entrance to the forest immediately. He then started to walk downhill toward Ismet's house. As he approached Ismet's house, another soldier with a torch ran past him to set fire to the house. He stopped the soldier, asked him to hand over the torch, and ordered him to go up the hill to the rendezvous point.

As the soldier ran up the hill, Burhan threw away the torch and turned toward the young girl. "I have to make sure this house is not burned down," he said. "I'll walk you in now. Inside, find a safe corner to hide and keep quiet until everyone has gone. Then go to the kitchen and look for a cellar door on the floor under an old kilim. Before you open it, announce yourself. Otherwise, you might get shot."

When Burhan turned around to guide the young girl into the house, he came face-to-face with Lieutenant Michailovitch.

"Burhan, you are a lucky bastard!" Michailovitch said. "You found yourself a beauty. Come on; let's go back to the camp! We are running late."

Burhan realized that he had no choice but to follow Lieutenant Michailovitch's entourage of a few soldiers and several young women who were being herded toward a terrible fate. Still gripping Nurjahan's arm, Burhan whispered to her in Turkish to be calm and quiet. As they walked up the hill, he saw that tears were pouring down her rosy cheeks. He reassured Nurjahan that no one would harm her.

The Convoy Under Threat

The day after the attacks, the evacuation convoy slowly continued its journey to Skopje with no further incidents. Before sunset, they made camp in a flat open area in a small valley not far from the Macedonian town of Tetovo. Under a cloudless, twinkling night sky, the convoy's members helped the soldiers prepare the evening meal.

After a container with their share of meal was delivered, Jemal and Servet ate scanty helpings of lentil mush and dried bread. Completing his meal, Jemal washed and put away the metal container. He then asked Servet's permission to leave. When she inquired why, he replied, "I must speak with Lieutenant Nihad about the overall security situation around the camp."

Before letting him go, Servet further inquired, "Lieutenant Nihad, where's he from?"

"I think he's from Istanbul."

"I should have guessed from his accent," Servet said. "Yes, Jemal, go ahead and give him my regards. If you can, please find out when we can expect to arrive at Skopje. Don't be long. I don't feel safe being alone after what happened this morning."

Failing to find the lieutenant in his tent, Jemal located him at the end of the convoy next to a wooded area. He was talking to a soldier who tightly held the reins of a white stallion. It appeared that the soldier had just arrived after a long ride. Jemal leaned against a tree trunk, waiting for his turn to talk with the lieutenant. Once the soldier led the stallion away, Jemal cautiously approached the lieutenant. Saluting, he asked permission to speak.

"What is it, Jemal?"

"Lieutenant, I'd like to know when we'll reach Skopje. Will it be tomorrow?"

Nihad looked slightly nervous and agitated. "Jemal," he said. "I cannot give you a precise answer, but I can tell you this much: I just had a long talk with one of the soldiers on rear guard duty, and he informed me that the enemy is approaching our convoy. During his late-afternoon reconnaissance, he noticed a group of fifty nationalist soldiers moving in our direction. I ordered him to select ten men to form a defense perimeter a few kilometers northwest of us. We can't afford a surprise attack in the morning. While they're fighting the enemy soldiers, we should be able to make it to Skopje by midday tomorrow, provided that our convoy moves before dawn. In one hour, the staff sergeant will inform you and others about the details of tomorrow morning's activities."

Jemal saluted the lieutenant and turned around to walk back to the cart. His head was spinning; he was frightened by a possible Serbian attack. He decided to have a talk with Selim about such a threatening possibility.

When Jemal entered the tent, Selim was talking to his grandson. "My little lion," Selim said to the child. "God willing, I'll tell you the rest of the story tomorrow night. Now go to your aunt's tent." The young boy left his grandfather's tent with a happy smile.

As Jemal said his usual respectful greetings to the old man, he sat on the colorful Turkish kilim spread on the ground.

Without waiting for him to start the conversation, Selim asked, "What ails you, my young brother?"

Jemal told Selim that the news he had heard earlier from the lieutenant was so frightening that he felt obliged to discuss it with someone. After providing the details, Jemal said, "Selim Efendi, I don't know what to do. I think I should leave the convoy early in the morning with the family I am responsible for. We could take a shortcut over the hills, which would allow us to reach Skopje more quickly and safely. What do you think?"

After a long pause, Selim responded, "That might be the safest way to reach Skopje, but I don't think the lieutenant will appreciate you taking such an action on your own initiative."

"I know the lieutenant will be disturbed when he finds out that we've left the convoy, but I really think this is the only way I can secure the safety of the family I'm responsible for. I owe this to Lieutenant Avni. I've made up my mind. Tomorrow, we'll leave two hours before dawn. Selim Baba, in the morning, I need you to provide cover for me by creating some sort of distraction for the guards, so they won't prevent us from leaving the convoy."

Selim got up, reached out and held Jemal's shoulders with both hands. "Rest assured, my young brother," he said affectionately. "We'll divert the attention of the guards to our camp. Then you can pull away with no problem. May God protect you and the family in your care. God willing, we'll soon see each other in Skopje."

A Camp of Cruelty

When they reached the designated camping area in a secluded corner of the forest, Lieutenant Michailovitch told everyone to settle down and rest. Burhan held Nurjahan by the arm and discreetly pulled her away from the center of the camp. He intended to let Nurjahan escape during the night to join Dursun and his family.

After finding a secluded area at the far edge of the camp, he placed the camping gear near a tree trunk and then untied Nurjahan's hands. "Please, relax and remain quiet," he said firmly. "Before we settle in this spot, we should wait for others to pitch their tents. I want to make sure no one is too close to us."

The young girl was shivering. Burhan removed a blanket from his camping bag and draped it over her shoulders. Nurjahan, eyes downcast, thanked him. "You haven't told me your name," she whispered. "But I've heard the Serbian officer call you Burhan. You are a Muslim, aren't you?"

"Yes, I'm a Muslim," Burhan said. Unwilling to say anything more, he changed the subject. "Would you like to help me pitch the tent? It's a small tent for one person. You'll have to share it with me. We must pretend that you are my ..." He stopped talking. He simply couldn't bring himself to say the word 'woman'.

Noticing Burhan's sudden confusion, Nurjahan looked up at him. "I understand, Sergeant. I'll play the part. What will happen to the other girls?"

Burhan, searching for the right words, remained silent for a while. He then spoke: "They will be raped tonight and possibly murdered in the morning."

The young girl began sobbing. "But why?" she asked. "What have they done to deserve such cruelty?"

"Nurjahan, I don't know why some men behave the way they do during war. Maybe it happens because of the complete breakdown of human reasoning and compassion. But one thing I know for sure is that both sides of this conflict conduct similar atrocities, particularly against young women."

Nurjahan, childishly, asked, "Can't you do anything to help them?"

"Myself? Alone?" Burhan responded briskly, "That would be suicide, but I hope I can at least save you."

Nurjahan turned her head away abruptly. "But you didn't prevent the murder of my brother."

Remembering every detail of the incident, Burhan answered, "Your brother killed one of our soldiers before he was shot. If we hadn't killed him, he would have killed more of us."

He then asked her to get up and help him unfold the tent. After the tent was set up, he told Nurjahan that he would leave her alone for a short while to get something to eat. Earlier, during the raid, soldiers had looted some food items from the village houses before burning them to the ground. After he lit a couple of candles, he gave Nurjahan a canteen full of water and cautioned, "If anyone comes by the tent, just keep quiet. If they come into the tent, tell them that you're my woman. Do you speak enough Serbo-Croatian to say that?" After she nodded, Burhan continued, "Just try keeping them away from you by talking to them. Do not fight or scream. I'll be back as quickly as I can."

In the pitch darkness, Burhan rushed toward the large bonfire in the middle of the camp-ground where most of the tents had been set up. While he looked for the pile of food that had been brought from the village, he saw several young women being dragged into tents. Despite the violence going on all around, the camp was strangely quiet. He kept walking around until he located the makeshift kitchen where several soldiers were preparing meals. He picked up some loaves of bread, chunks of cheese, and boiled potatoes. Arms loaded with food, he turned to leave the kitchen.

He stopped abruptly when one of the soldiers shouted, "Sergeant, a short while ago the lieutenant was asking about your tent's whereabouts."

In response, Burhan asked the soldier where the lieutenant's tent was. The soldier pointed to a large, double-sized tent next to the flaming bonfire. Burhan then ordered the soldier to tell the lieutenant that he would be there in ten minutes.

Burhan ran back to his tent and handed the armload of food to Nurjahan. "I've got to leave again," he said hurriedly. "It may be a while before I return. Feed yourself."

As he was leaving, he reminded her, "If anyone comes, you should do everything possible to keep yourself alive." Without waiting for a response, he disappeared into the darkness.

Lieutenant Michailovitch warmly welcomed Burhan to his tent. The spacious canvas tent was remarkably warm and reeked of body odor. The source of heat was the red-hot charcoal container placed near the entry. The strong body odor had been generated by heavy sweating. Hearing a deep moan coming from the rear of the tent, Burhan realized that the lieutenant had just completed his entertainment for the night.

As he straightened his trousers with one hand, Michailovitch clung to the wooden post in the center of the tent with the other. He was highly intoxicated. "Are you enjoying yourself with your young Turkish woman?" he mumbled.

Burhan forced a smile and said, "Yes, very much so Lieutenant. I was told that you wanted to see me."

"We lost five men this afternoon; two from your company. Tell me what happened."

For the next few minutes, Burhan explained how and where he had lost the two men. For obvious reasons, he did not admit shooting one of them. He invented a heroic story about the death of that particular soldier.

Michailovitch, still leaning on the tent's center post, listened closely to every word with great intensity and then brusquely told Burhan to be more careful with the men under his command. "I'll be watching you during the coming battles," he hissed.

After a few more words of advice, Michailovitch told Burhan to walk with him to the end of the tent. A young woman was lying atop several layers of thick woolen blankets spread on the ground. Her body was covered with a large army overcoat.

Bending forward, the lieutenant held a candle closer to the moaning figure shivering under the coat, and sneered, "Look at this beast! Isn't she beautiful?"

He reached down and jerked the army coat off the young woman, uncovering her completely naked body. She was bound and gagged; her eyes were red and badly swollen. Her elbows were tied to her ankles behind her body, forcing her legs to bend outward at the knees. Her breasts and genitals were completely exposed. She was clearly in great pain and shock from this cruel treatment.

The horrendous sight made Burhan feel that he was about to gag. He turned around to avoid looking at such extreme cruelty. "But why, Lieutenant?" he plaintively asked.

"Earlier this evening, one of the Albanian girls almost gouged out the eye of a soldier as he was raping her," Michailovitch answered. "So, at the suggestion of the sergeant, we have decided to take the necessary precautions. It's much safer this way."

"What happened to the girl who resisted the rape?"

"She was cut to pieces by the soldier. By the way, how are you handling your Turkish delight?"

Burhan lied, "She's tied up as well, but just her hands."

"Doesn't she kick your ass?" asked Michailovitch mockingly.

Sick and tired of this conversation, Burhan replied, "I like it that way!" Then he quickly asked, "What's going to happen to these women, Lieutenant?"

"We'll let them go back to their village in the morning," Michailovitch replied casually. "They can tell all the Muslim villagers in southern Kosovo that we intend to get rid of them once and for all."

Enraged, Burhan made his way back to his tent. Cursing Michailovitch, he muttered in Albanian, "I would love to put a bullet in his brain." As he approached his tent, he heard noises coming from inside. He unsheathed his knife, placed it between his jaws, threw himself on the ground, and crawled toward the entrance to the tent. He pushed aside the canvas flap, and saw the silhouette of a soldier on top of Nurjahan. She was loudly begging the soldier to stop in Serbo-Croatian. Burhan very cautiously and quietly slipped into the tent, grabbed the man by the hair, and laid the razor-sharp blade on his throat. "If you make a move or a sound, I'll cut your throat," he whispered into the soldier's ear. He then forcefully jerked the soldier out of the tent and rammed him down on the ground on his belly. With his knee planted firmly on the soldier's back and the knife still at the soldier's throat, he asked Nurjahan if she was all right.

As she peered through the open canvas flap, Nurjahan replied in a voice trembling with fear and relief, "I'm glad you've returned in time. I'm not hurt. What will you do with him?"

Burhan did not answer. Instead, he yanked the soldier to his feet and turned him toward the camp fire in the distance. He hoarsely hollered, "Stay away from my woman. If I see you near my tent again, I'll kill you. Now get lost!" He watched the young soldier stumble away toward the camp fire. Sheathing his knife, he entered the tent and lit a candle.

Nurjahan was fumbling in haste to put her clothes back on.

"If you had arrived one minute later, that animal would have raped me."

Burhan asked again, "Are you all right?"

"Yes and no!" Nurjahan replied, differently this time.

He knew what she meant. "Try to get some sleep," he said. "You'll have another tough day tomorrow. You should be rested for your escape in the morning."

Nurjahan lay down and pulled the blanket over her head. Burhan, sitting on the ground, retrieved the piece of bread and cheese that had been thrown to the back of the tent during the struggle with the intruder. Hungrily, he bit into a large piece of bread. As he felt and tasted gritty dirt in his mouth, he quickly spat it out and searched for his canteen. He pulled out the cork to take a drink of water and, subconsciously, began to do something he had not done for a long time: he started to pray.

A few hours later, Burhan awoke and gently touched Nurjahan's shoulder, urging her to wake up. After telling her to get ready quickly, he left the tent to check on the night guards positioned at camp's periphery. After surveying the grounds for a short while, he decided to lead Nurjahan on a path between two snoring guards. He retrieved her from the tent and told her to follow him quietly.

In the middle of the night, they walked side by side in silence like two friendly ghosts moving through the darkness of the forest. As soon as they had reached the edge of the woods, Burhan stopped and turned toward her. "This is where we separate," he whispered. "Do you remember the house I told you about yesterday?"

"Yes, I remember. It's the house of the village headman."

"You're a smart girl. Be very careful going down the hill in the dark. When you reach the house, find the entrance to the cellar in the kitchen. Before opening the cellar hatch, announce yourself loudly; otherwise, you will face Dursun's pistol. In the cellar, you will find him and his family. Tell Dursun to leave immediately for Skopje. May the Lord protect all of you!"

Burhan hunkered down against a large tree trunk, watching her walk down the hill. When she disappeared into darkness, he murmured to himself, "I'd like to see her again." As if in a dream, he slowly walked back inside the tent, and lay flat on his back. Smelling the sweet scent of Nurjahan on the blanket, he quickly fell asleep.

The Fifteenth of January: Leaving the Convoy

Servet cautiously pushed aside the canvas flap to peek outside. She could see nothing; it was pitch dark. She lit a candle and held it out of the canvas to see what was happening. Jemal was harnessing the mule.

The glimmer of candle caught Jemal's eye. He rushed to the cart and blew the candle out. "Madam," he whispered. "Candlelight at this time of night may jeopardize our departure. As we move away from the camp, please do everything you can to keep little Bedia quiet. We'll leave in ten minutes."

Once the mule was harnessed, Jemal threw his bag into the cart and positioned himself in front of the animal. Gathering the reins, he gently stroked the mule's head. He was waiting for Selim's signal. Within minutes, a young boy from the Turkish villagers' camp crept quietly behind the cart and softly called Jemal's name. That was the agreed-upon signal indicating all was well.

Just before pulling away from the camp, Jemal remembered to grease the wooden axles to prevent their squeaking. Because of that, the reins kept slipping from his oily fingers. Grabbing the reins tightly with both hands, Jemal coaxed the mule slowly out of the camp toward the northern hills.

The cart quietly moved along the snow-covered ground and soon reached the gentle slopes north of the campground. Thirty minutes later, it crested the first slope. Stopping the cart, Jemal turned to take a last look at the campground below. He could barely detect the shadowy outlines of the carts and wagons lined up next to each other. He whispered prayers for the well-being of the compatriots he was leaving behind, and for a safe passage on the dangerous journey he was about to undertake.

Jemal walked back to the cart. "Servet Hanim, Servet Hanim," he whispered excitedly. "We've made it. We're on our way to Skopje. I think we'll be there before noon."

Servet pushed the canvas flap aside and handed Jemal a metal plate with cheese and bread. "While you were on guard duty last night, this was delivered to me by Selim Baba."

Jemal thanked her and gratefully took the plate. Leaning against the big wooden cartwheel, he tore off a large bite of the fresh bread. As he chewed hurriedly, he wondered about his own upcoming trip home. *But first, we must reach Skopje,* he mused.

The Battle

Avni received his final instructions from the regimental commander: in the early morning hours of the next day, his unit was to provide rear guard protection to the heavy artillery units being withdrawn. The following day, the Yanyevo troops were to move toward northeastern plains to strengthen the right flank of retreating infantry and cavalry regiments heading away from the enemy positions at Pudujevo. A day earlier, Avni had joined a reconnaissance mission to assess the safety of an ongoing artillery withdrawal. During the reconnaissance, he had noted the presence of many heavy artillery units under the protection of sizeable cavalry and infantry regiments moving toward their final destination, the town of Kumanovo in southeastern Kosovo.

Pulling his stallion Yagiz behind him, Lieutenant Avni led his men down the Tepe Hills, through a valley that ended in a gorge connected to the plains of northeastern Kosovo. With the exception of four soldiers who had been taken ill, all one hundred and forty men were closely following the lieutenant. Most of the men were regular soldiers who had been wounded during the earlier skirmishes and recovered in Yanyevo's hospital. The rest were hospital staff and a few untrained local recruits.

Just before reaching the gorge, which led to the open plains, Avni ordered his men to halt. He took out his field glasses and carefully scanned the horizon. At this early hour of the morning, he did not expect that there would be anything threatening to observe. *Unless*, he reasoned, *the enemy had ridden all night to catch up with the retreating Ottoman heavy-artillery regiment.*

Suddenly, he froze. Straining his neck forward, he hollered, "God damn it!" He usually did not curse in front of his men. Turning sharply around, he ordered silence and motioned for the staff sergeant to come next to him with his own field glasses. For a moment they both scrutinized the horizon, hoping that what they had seen was an illusion.

The sergeant, still holding the field glasses fixed on the horizon, whispered, "Sir, this is a sizeable Serbian cavalry regiment moving rather rapidly toward us. I estimate they'll reach the gorge in two hours. We must stop them here. We have no choice but to prevent them from reaching the tail end of the units withdrawing to Kumanovo."

Avni lowered his field glasses. "We are a small force, Sergeant," he said sullenly. "Our cavalry regiment in Pristina is large enough to counter this Serbian attack on our retreating artillery units. The Pristina cavalry is scheduled to enter the plains from the southwest by seven o'clock, a little over an hour from now."

Avni ordered the sergeant to gather the troop leaders for new instructions. As they were gathering, Lieutenant Avni loudly called for young Avni, who quickly appeared in front of him.

"Young man," the lieutenant ordered. "Get a good horse; ride as fast as you can toward the advance-cavalry unit moving from Pristina toward Pudujevo in northeastern Kosovo. If you are fast, you may meet the cavalry a few kilometers north of the Pristina defense area. While you prepare, I'll write a note to the commander of the cavalry. You must hand him the note personally."

A short while later, Avni came out of his tent, handed an envelope to the young soldier, and ordered him to leave immediately. He then joined the sergeant and the troop leaders who were sitting on the ground waiting for him. He sat next to the sergeant and began speaking. "An enemy cavalry unit of more than six hundred men is expected to reach the Tepe Hills gorge within an hour. Given the size of our unit, we may not be able to stop them. But, because we are in a gorge, we can definitely slow them down. The enemy must not be allowed to reach our heavy artillery convoy. If the enemy passes through the ravine and reaches them, they could destroy our army's main defense capacity."

Avni laid a large map of the Tepe Hills on the ground. "Let me explain what we are about to do," he said sternly. "I've sent a messenger to the commander of our advance cavalry regiment moving north from the Field of Blackbirds. I asked him to divert some of his cavalrymen here to the Tepe Hills gorge as reinforcements. I estimate they'll arrive here within two or three hours at the most. That leaves us facing the enemy alone for more than an hour. If we can hold the nationalist cavalry for that long here at the entrance to the gorge, our reinforcements will surprise the enemy cavalry from the rear. If everything goes according to plan, we could destroy them. Now, the main issue that we have to discuss is how we can detain the enemy here at the gorge until reinforcements arrive."

After a short pause, Lieutenant Avni continued, "I'll lead a surprise attack with fifty men on horseback. We'll attack them precisely when the enemy cavalry reaches the first sharp bend in the gorge, approximately two hundred fifty meters from the main entrance. Because of the narrowness of that part of the gorge, only about twelve enemy cavalrymen can enter at a time. At that curve, we'll be waiting for them. Our surprise attack will be supported by seventy infantry soldiers led by the sergeant. The infantry will attack the enemy from each flank. The remaining twenty men will establish themselves in the higher reaches of the gorge: ten sharpshooters in each flank. They'll fire continuously on the enemy. I hope that we'll be able to pin them down for an hour or longer. These are your instructions; now prepare yourselves for the battle."

As he finished giving these instructions, Avni realized the basic weakness in his strategy. Remembering the battle strategy training he had received at the war academy, he thought, *If I can plan a surprise attack in the gorge, I'm sure the enemy has also planned a strategy to insure peripheral security.* He jumped to his feet and ordered the sergeant to select twenty good fighters from the regular infantry troops.

"Sergeant, we must confront an enemy advance reconnaissance unit moving toward us at this very moment. Prepare your men to attack the main enemy column as planned. Of the twenty men I am taking with me to the hills, some may be able to return shortly to join you in battle, if they survive the onslaught of the intruders. In my absence, you're in charge of the troops in the gorge. God protect us all and give us the strength to stop the enemy."

Avni ordered the twenty handpicked soldiers to line up. He chose two older, experienced soldiers to check the presence of the enemy reconnaissance infantry on the left flank of the gorge. He gave them specific instructions. "Take position on a well-hidden high point," he ordered. "Watch the immediate surroundings and the northern horizon constantly. If you notice enemy activity in the immediate area, you should pull back and one of you must report to me immediately. You'll find me at the end of the eastern ridge. The other one must inform the sergeant and the troops in the gorge. God protect both of you!"

Avni took the remaining eighteen men with him to do exactly the same thing on the opposite side of the gorge. Because of its gentler slopes, Avni had expected that there would be an expeditionary infantry unit on the eastern ridge to secure the enemy cavalry's entry into the ravine. However, in case he was wrong, one of the two men on the western ridge would hopefully inform him in time for a quick reassessment of the situation.

At the end of the ravine, where the hills met the plains, Avni positioned himself high on the eastern ridge, which provided him an unobstructed view of the entrance to the narrow pass. Browsing the horizon with his field glasses, at first he saw no suspicious activity at all. Suddenly, however, he spotted a group horses tied to a tree near the hillside. Moving the field glasses toward the hill below, he saw the enemy soldiers climbing up toward them. He counted ten men hurriedly scrambling up the hill to reach the top to determine the safety of the pass. He thought, *If they notice our presence, they will warn the cavalry column not to enter the ravine. Then a large number of cavalrymen on foot will attack us to secure positions on both flanks, thereby assuring safe passage for the nationalist cavalry through the narrow pass of the ravine.*

Avni suddenly realized the need to quickly decide what type of action his troops should take on this small advance enemy unit. He knew he had only a few choices. He could let the enemy unit proceed and then attack them from behind. *Ten of them against nineteen of us,* he mused. *We can easily eliminate them all.*

Somehow he felt this was not the best strategy. He deemed that killing most of the enemy soldiers, but not all of them was a wiser strategy. The surviving soldiers could then alert their cavalry. That would definitely bring the enemy cavalry to a halt before they had entered the gorge. However, time was against this option.

What if, Avni pondered, *the main nationalist cavalry column reaches the gorge before we are able to destroy the expeditionary unit?*

Even though there were greater risks to his men, Avni decided that the best option was to immediately attack the enemy soldiers while they climbed the hill, killing most of them and letting a few escape to alert the enemy cavalry column that the ravine was defended by Ottoman forces. He was convinced that this strategy would bring the enemy cavalry to a definite halt. The Serbians would then quickly convert some of the cavalry into infantry in order to secure the peripheral flanks of the pass before commencing the cavalry attack into the ravine. Avni was sure that this delay would buy time for the Pristina reinforcements to attack the rear of the halted nationalist cavalry.

Lieutenant Avni ordered his troops to spread out and prepare to snipe at the enemy soldiers. He cautioned, "Wait until I fire the first shot. Then keep on firing until you kill most of them. We have to let a few enemy soldiers escape."

As he scanned the immediate landscape for any enemy soldier presence, he leaned on a large boulder, and cocked his rifle to shoot at the first nationalist soldier who appeared on the steep hillside below him. There he was! A nationalist soldier, about fifty meters below, was laboring hard to climb the rugged, steep hill in front of him. Avni's heart was pounding. He aimed and pulled the trigger. The boom of the gunshot echoed widely and bounced off the hillsides. As he blinked repeatedly to clear his vision, which had been blurred by the powerful kick of the rifle butt against his shoulder, Avni saw the enemy soldier fall backward, his arms pinwheeling in the air as if he wanted to fly. Avni's shot was immediately followed by thunderous salvos fired from the rifles of his men. He noticed several enemy soldiers take positions in preparation to fire back. But most of them had been wounded and the ones remaining in good shape slipped and skidded down the hill. Avni ran to the nearest soldier, calling out the order to cease fire. For another minute or two, gunshots continued. As the sudden eerie silence descended on the ridge, he returned to the boulder and peered down the hill with his field glasses. He saw three enemy soldiers on horses racing northwest to meet the incoming Serbian cavalry.

Avni whispered, "So far, so good. Now, what is next?" He ordered ten soldiers to remain on the eastern ridge and to prepare to defend it. He told the most senior soldier to take command of the unit. The remaining eight men followed him down the hill and into the ravine. As they reached the narrow gorge, Avni ordered the eight men to join the two soldiers already on the western ridge. As the men ran to the other side of the ravine, he walked briskly toward the sharp curve where the remaining Yanyevo troops were positioned.

The sergeant ran toward him, shouting, "Lieutenant, what happened? We heard shots coming from the hills. Are you all right?"

As they walked back to where the troops were, Avni told the sergeant what had happened on the eastern ridge. "I left a ten-man team on each ridge to contain the enemy infantry attacks on the flanks. That leaves us with seventy infantry soldiers and fifty cavalrymen here in the gorge. I will lead the fifty men on horseback to face the enemy cavalry just where the bend begins to curve sharply. Immediately send ten sharpshooters to each flank. Instruct them not to shoot into the main battle area. If they do that, they will also hit our soldiers. They must concentrate their shots on the enemy cavalry soldiers who are trying to negotiate the sharp curve. The remaining fifty infantry soldiers, under your guidance, should enter the battle from both flanks immediately after our cavalry has engaged the enemy. I believe we will be able to hold the Serbians long enough for our reinforcements to attack the enemy from the rear. God willing, Sergeant, today's victory will be ours."

Avni quickly inspected the troops' readiness with the sergeant by his side, and then climbed back up the hillside to scrutinize the horizon. Peering through the field glasses, he estimated that the enemy cavalry would reach the gorge in less than half an hour.

"Now they know we're here to fight them," he muttered. A panicky feeling started to overwhelm him and a sudden fear of death began to cloud Avni's judgment and muddle his mind. Feeling the rush of adrenalin, he slumped to the ground, put his head on his knees, and prayed over and over again, "God willing, I will survive to see my wife and child."

He straightened up, adjusted his uniform, and descended to the narrow pass for final preparations. Mounting Yagiz, Avni ordered his cavalrymen to fall back once the initial confrontation was over, then regroup and attack again, and again. He instructed the infantry troop leaders to do the same.

"Back up into the hills after the initial attack, then regroup and attack again at the same time as the cavalry." He repeated his earlier order to the sharpshooters positioned on the flanks, telling them to fire continuously at the enemy to slow them down. "You must aim at the enemy cavalry soldiers at the periphery. Don't fire into the main battle area."

As he heard gunshots from both sides of the ridge, he prayed that his men could successfully keep the enemy at bay. Otherwise, his troops in the gorge would become moving targets for the enemy infantry. Avni heard the thunder of horse hooves as the enemy cavalry prepared to enter the narrow pass. He slowly pulled his sword from its sheath. The sounds of the blades chafing against their sheaths filled the air as all fifty cavalrymen drew steel in unison. Avni held his sword aloft for a moment, and then brought it down, poised with the pommel at his chin and the blade pointing toward the sky. Moving the tip of the blade down in the direction of the oncoming enemy, he shouted with all his strength, "In the name of our sovereign, we are ready to spill our blood for our country. May merciful God grant us victory!"

SPARKS
OF
HOPE

The Fifteenth of January: Servet in the Forest

Servet cradled her infant, who was swaddled in layers of soft blankets. She gazed with loving eyes at her infant daughter, so healthy and so beautiful. Little Bedia had her father's dark, almond-shaped eyes. Her hair was thick and black, just like Avni's. Her skin was pale and smooth. "Just like mine!" Servet said. Most importantly, Servet felt that Bedia was an even-tempered, good-natured baby; she did not cry much, unless hungry or uncomfortable. Servet looked deep into her baby's eyes. She was full of loving thoughts: *I love you so much, my precious one. God willing, I'll have more children like you.*

Suddenly, she heard Jemal grumbling and loudly complaining outside the cart. She peeked through the denim flaps. From behind the mule's rump, she saw Jemal pulling the reins of the exhausted mule with both hands as it struggled to haul the cart up the steep hill. Servet looked around to see where they were: passing through a thick and lush evergreen forest, which appeared peaceful and captivatingly beautiful. Snow fully blanketed the ground, and snowflakes graced the tall, elegant trees. Comforted by the peacefulness of the nature surrounding her, Servet wondered why so much hatred and malice existed among people. "Why can't we share this beautiful land and coexist in peace and tranquility?" she murmured.

In order to be heard over the loud, incessant squeak of the wooden axles, she yelled out, "Jemal, how much longer until we reach Skopje?"

Without stopping or turning his head, Jemal replied, "We may have a couple more hours of travel. How is little Bedia doing?"

"She's doing very well," replied Servet. "Do you think we can afford to stop and take a break for a few minutes?"

Stopping the mule, Jemal turned around. "Of course, madam, we can stop for a short while. Please remember, we've to get out of harm's way as quickly as we can. The closer we get to Skopje, the safer we are. These hills are full of renegade irregular soldiers and deserters from both sides. These dangerous characters have no mercy. They would kill anyone just for food and clothing. We're almost at the top of this long climb. From now on we'll travel on flat land until we reach Skopje."

After securing her baby safely in a well-cushioned corner, Servet climbed from the cart onto the snow-covered ground.

"I've got to walk down the hill to check if we're being followed," Jemal said to Servet as he helped her step off the cart. He had decided to walk away from the cart so that Servet could have some privacy. He trotted quickly down the hill and turned left toward the steep ledge. He gazed over the territory through which they had traveled since the early morning. At this height, he was able to see most of the rolling hills he and the mule had painstakingly climbed. Suddenly, at the top of the third hilltop below where he stood, he saw a couple of horses tied to trees. He saw two men in army coats in the open field next to the horses. From this distance he could not identify their uniforms. It appeared that they were both standing still and looking in his direction. It appeared that one of them was using field glasses.

Jemal was overwhelmed by a sudden anxiety. A swift, nerve-racking fear filled his mind. *If they have seen us,* he contemplated, *and if they need something we have, such as food or ammunition, they could catch up with us within an hour or less.*

He whirled around and ran toward the cart. As he rushed to the cart, he called out to Servet. She immediately answered him, "I'm back, Jemal. I was wondering about you. You told me to hurry up, so I got back as quickly as I could. You were gone much longer than I expected!"

He hurriedly explained, "Madam, we've got to move quickly. I saw two uniformed men, a couple of renegades or deserters either from the enemy or from our side. They're traveling toward us from the western hills and could overtake us in less than an hour. We must reach the plains immediately. While we climb the hill, I will think of a way to fend off these two drifters."

He pulled the reins, jerking the head of the mule forward to start the cart moving. In less than fifteen minutes, he had reached the top of the hill and begun traveling on the open plains, which stretched all the way to Skopje. Estimating that they were an hour's travel from the city, Jemal stopped the cart and asked Servet to get out of the cart with her baby. He took the cart's harness off the mule to free the animal. He then reached into the cart, grabbed several blankets and a small container with food and water. He threw the blankets over the mule's back and put the small container on the ground. Holding the reins in one hand, he took the baby from Servet. With little Bedia in his left arm, he helped Servet up onto the mule.

While she was struggling to sit on the animal's back, Servet commented, "Thank God Avni taught me how to ride a horse."

"Mules are slower and easier to control," Jemal said as he handed the baby up to her. After handing her the small container with food and water he took the compass from his side pocket and gave it to her. "Servet Hanim," he said. "I hope you know how to use this."

"I've seen Avni's compass around the house. The arrow points to the north, right?"

Jemal was pleased. "Yes," he replied, "but you'll travel southeast. Do you see the letters SE on the right bottom side of the compass?"

When she nodded, Jemal handed her the reins and gave her final instructions. "Servet Hanim, please ride the mule in the direction I showed you. Don't look back. Go as fast as you can. In an hour or so you will reach the city. Once there, you'll know what to do. God protect you and your baby."

Jemal smacked the mule's rump to get it going.

Servet turned toward Jemal and shouted, "God bless and protect you. I hope to see you soon in Skopje."

After watching the mule trot away over the snowy ground, Jemal returned to the cart. He picked up his rifle and slung it over his shoulder, checked his revolver for bullets, and put it back in the holster. He reached into the metal storage box and grabbed a handful of extra bullets, putting them into his side pockets. He then pulled the water container off the cart and poured water into his empty canteen. Still holding the canteen in his hand, he slowly walked backward on the snow-covered track of the cartwheel. When he approached the edge of the forest, he suddenly stopped, turned sideways, and moved forward toward a group of large trees nearby. After every few steps, he stretched his strides, and every few steps he turned around to cover his footprints with snow. Satisfied that his tracks were concealed, he reached the group of trees. Ducking behind the largest tree, he placed his gear down on the ground, and removed his rifle. He double-checked that it was loaded, cocked it into firing position, and leaned it against the tree trunk. He nervously took his revolver out and rechecked its chambers. After verifying that it was also fully loaded, he placed it in the holster.

Earlier, while pulling the cart uphill, he had carefully selected this location as a place to wait for the uniformed drifters who were following them. From this vantage point, he could see down the hill where the renegades, he hoped, would appear. He decided he would let them pass him by and approach the cart. When they had reached the cart, Jemal hoped they would stop to check what it contained. If they attempted to follow the mule's tracks to catch up with Servet, he would shoot them, but he did not think they would follow. Finding the cart alone, the soldiers would assume they had escaped on the mule. Jemal was sure that the renegades would first rob the cart, and then just go away. He was confident that what he had set up was a safe plan. He did not want to kill anyone unless he absolutely had to. He braced himself against the tree trunk and quietly hummed one of his favorite folk songs.

Revisiting Selim's Village

As they were galloping away from the smoldering village they had destroyed, Michailovitch turned to Burhan. "This morning we did better than yesterday. We left no one alive in the village. We lost only one man. This has been a very good morning, indeed. But we're too early for the Pristina gathering this afternoon." Turning his attention to the sergeant riding on his left, Michailovitch hollered, "Why don't we destroy another village?"

Before the sergeant could respond, Burhan replied, "There's a large Turkish village close by. I noticed it during my secret mission last week." Burhan was referring to the Turkish village where he and Ismet had pretended to be Ottoman officers supporting the relocation of Turkish villages. He was sure there would be no one remaining in the village. Since a detour to the deserted Turkish village would take the rest of the morning, such a diversion would prevent Michailovitch from attacking yet another village.

With a serious demeanor, Burhan looked at the lieutenant and said, "I'll lead you there."

They reached Selim's village by noon. When he realized they were entering a completely empty village, Michailovitch went berserk. He raged and cursed Burhan, who calmly ignored the insults. Since there was nothing else to be done, they dismounted and looked for a place to have their midday meal. They sat around an old wooden table in the vacant coffeehouse.

During the meal Burhan heard the lieutenant say, "Somehow I'm relieved to see these Turkish villages empty. After five hundred years, the Turks are finally going home. We should torch the entire village. They'll never be able to return."

Burhan walked away from his comrades to control his temper and to have a few minutes of solitude. He walked toward the small masjid behind which he noticed a small, well-kept Muslim cemetery dotted with engraved marble head stones, some of which boasted fancy carvings of fezes or turbans. Once inside the cemetery, Burhan leaned against a large headstone that probably marked the grave of one of the former dignitaries of the village.

He unexpectedly began remembering the tragedies and heartaches of his youth. His mother had died when he was a little boy of ten. Katya had been murdered when he was a young man of nineteen. Now, at the age of twenty-two, he had lost his only brother and felt certain he was about to lose his father.

Where is Father now? Burhan wondered. *What could he be doing at this very moment? If he is still in Pristina, I must find him and take him home away from this misery.*

He heard the wind blow gently through the branches of the towering cypress trees that always marked the perimeter of Turkish cemeteries. His thoughts drifted toward Nurjahan. He hoped, from the bottom of his heart, that she was safely on her way to Skopje. A flicker of flame caught his eye; his comrades had already started burning houses. He walked out of the cemetery to join them and do his share of the damage. The smoke-filled air bitterly reminded him of the scene from the previous village. This time, at least, he could console himself with the thought that no one had been killed. A soldier in the street told Burhan to report to the lieutenant, who was lounging in the coffeehouse one block away.

Burhan nonchalantly entered the old, rundown wooden shack. Michailovitch ordered him to take a seat near his table. Burhan sat precariously on a wobbly old stool.

"Lieutenant," Burhan said calmly. "I think you have a challenging new assignment for me."

Michailovitch, appearing preoccupied, answered, "Yes, listen carefully. I just received a message from the units waiting for us north of Pristina. This morning, one of our large cavalry regiments was attacked and destroyed by the Ottoman army south of the Tepe Hills. I want you to ride to Pudujevo to deliver a message to Commander Karaevitch. Take two men with you. Leave Pudujevo very early tomorrow morning. You must return to the meeting point at the outskirts of Pristina before we attack the town."

Renegades

A breeze gently caressed Jemal's cheek. He was having a hard time staying awake. He had slept barely three hours the previous night before he and Servet snuck out of the camp. More than an hour had passed since Servet and Bedia had begun the last portion of their journey to Skopje on mule back.

Servet Hanim should have reached Skopje by now, he thought. *The renegades should also have reached here by now. Maybe, I was wrong about those men following us. Possibly they lost our track.*

He got up, put the rifle on his shoulder, and slowly walked out of the woods toward the cart. He needed to take a few more food items with him before he could commence his long walk to Skopje. When he was halfway between the forest and the cart, he heard someone shout in Albanian, "Hey, Turk! Where are you going?"

As he pulled the rifle from his shoulder, Jemal whirled around to see where the call had come from. As the blasting sound of a rifle shot reached him, he spotted two horsemen dressed in ragged Ottoman uniforms. Just as he moved to throw himself on the ground, he felt a burning pain in his shoulder. Falling backward on the ground, Jemal hit his head on the edge of a rock, barely visible in the snow, and lost consciousness.

On the Way to Pudujevo

As ordered, Burhan and the two nationalist soldiers were riding fast on the plains toward the town of Pudujevo. Burhan saw the Tepe Hills on his right. Pointing to the distant hills, Burhan yelled to the soldier riding next to him.

"Is this the place where we lost a cavalry unit this morning?"

"No, sir! The cavalry battle took place at the southern end of the Tepe Hills, not here."

The other soldier suddenly called for Burhan's attention, "I see a man on horseback in the far distance. Look at ten o'clock northwest of us, Sergeant."

Burhan halted his horse. He quickly removed his field glasses from the leather pouch and focused on the fast-moving figure far ahead of them. He could see it was an Ottoman soldier, riding fast toward the northern part of the Tepe Hills. He ordered one of the soldiers known for being a good sharpshooter to get his rifle ready. They rode toward the galloping Ottoman soldier.

When they were within range, Burhan ordered the rifleman to shoot the horse, not the man.

The soldier argued, "For God's sake, Sergeant, why? Let me blow him away."

"Don't you wonder why he is riding alone through this no-man's-land in the middle of the day? We'll only find out what he is up to by making him talk. Just shoot the horse."

The rifleman dismounted, steadied himself in a proper position, and fired. Burhan saw the horse fall immediately on its side, throwing the rider forward. Ordering his men to follow him, Burhan rushed his horse toward the fallen soldier.

Burhan ordered a soldier near him to keep an eye on the enemy, who lay flat on his face. He quickly reached the badly wounded horse, and at once shot the suffering animal. He dismounted and walked toward the Ottoman soldier lying on the ground. Burhan pointed his revolver at the motionless body as the Serbian soldier behind him aimed his rifle at the Ottoman soldier's head. He carefully approached the soldier and slowly turned him on his back. He right away recognized the young recruit from Yanyevo, who appeared bruised but not badly hurt. "He has just been knocked out by the hard fall from his horse," Burhan murmured.

The presence of a member of the Yanyevo unit in the area compelled Burhan to think that his father could be nearby. He ordered one of his men to tie the enemy soldier's hands and feet. Burhan was now worried about the possibility of his townsman recognizing him. He told the men to take a rest while he interrogated the enemy soldier who was about to stir into consciousness.

Burhan sat on the hard ground next to young Avni and questioned him in Albanian. "Where are you rushing to, young man?"

Young Avni, still dazed, mumbled, "I was returning to my unit. What do you want from me? Why didn't you kill me? If I had had a chance, I would have killed you."

Obviously, the young man had not yet recognized Burhan. As he helped the soldier drink some water, Burhan leaned close and whispered into his ear. "My dear boy, if you want to stay alive, you must tell me where you are going. I believe you were traveling to your unit. Where are your comrades?"

Young Avni growled, "Why should I tell you?" Then, suddenly recognizing Burhan, he hissed, "You goddamn traitor! Why should I tell you anything?"

"Listen to me carefully. Let's be honest; you're interested in returning to your unit, and I'm interested in finding out about my father. Now, if you and I agree to cooperate, we'll both stay alive and accomplish what we want. If you don't agree to my proposal, I'll kill you now. Or, if you squeal later in front of the other soldiers, you'll get us both killed. So your best chance for survival is to cooperate with me. What do you say?"

Young Avni reluctantly nodded his head. "What exactly do you want me to do?"

"Just answer my questions. Where is the Yanyevo unit?"

"They're on the northern end of the Tepe Hills, right at the entrance to the gorge. They were supposed to launch a surprise attack on the nationalist cavalry this morning. I do not know what has happened since my departure. I was sent to deliver a message to the commander of the Ottoman cavalry regiment in Pristina. Lieutenant Avni asked for reinforcements to help him stop the Serbian cavalry. Unfortunately, the Ottoman cavalry was sent down to the southern end of the Tepe Hills to surprise the enemy cavalry. After hearing about this decision by the cavalry commander, I decided to go back to find out what had happened to my unit."

Burhan then told young Avni what he knew about the cavalry battle that had happened at the south end of the Tepe Hills. "In the early afternoon, a large Serbian cavalry regiment was destroyed by the Ottoman army at the southern end of the pass. Regrettably, this could mean that the small Yanyevo unit had been completely annihilated during the earlier confrontation. They all are probably dead by now, including my father."

As he stared at Burhan's face, young Avni said, "If you promise to let me go free, I'll tell you something of great interest to you."

Noticing that one of the nationalist soldiers was approaching him, Burhan turned and ordered the soldier to get ready to move. As the soldier moved away, he promised that he would set him free and urged young Avni to tell him what he had in his mind quickly.

"Your father is in Pristina," young Avni replied. "He was arrested by the Ottoman military intelligence. He is locked in a building next to the command center."

Relieved, Burhan took his knife out and moved closer to the young recruit.

Fearing for his life, the Ottoman soldier wailed, "You promised!"

Ignoring the outcry, Burhan cut the ropes binding young Avni's hands and whispered, "Keep your hands together as if they're still tied. Stay on the ground until we have disappeared over the horizon. As soon as I mount my horse, I'll shoot at you. Pretend you're hit and act as if you're dying."

Burhan rapidly joined the two soldiers waiting for him. After they had mounted their horses, Burhan snatched his rifle from the saddle and swung it onto his shoulder.

As they began riding away from young Avni, one of the soldiers asked, "Sergeant, aren't you going to shoot him?"

Burhan, as he swiveled in the saddle, replied, "Of course, I'll shoot the bastard." Aiming to miss, he slowly pulled the trigger. "A good hit!" shouted one of the soldiers.

Young Avni kept his face buried into the hard, dusty ground as he watched Burhan and the two nationalist soldiers disappear over the horizon. He then hurriedly untied his feet. After collecting as much food and water from his dead horse as he could carry, he pulled his rifle from the horse's underbelly. He slung the rifle over his shoulder and commenced walking rapidly toward the high hills. He was grateful to be alive. He knew that when he reached the gorge, his life would depend on finding a horse. He hoped that a few stray horses might still be around the battlefield. Without a horse, he had little chance of survival in enemy territory. As the silhouette of the sharply ridged hills rose up in the near distance, he broke into a slow run.

Servet in Skopje

Traveling alone, Servet was petrified at the thought of getting lost. Squinting to focus on the horizon, she felt tears of relief fill her eyes as she saw the cloudy silhouette of Skopje. During the last hour or so, she had seriously wondered where she was. She had diligently followed the southeast direction on the compass. Nonetheless, she felt completely alone and helpless as she and her baby made their way across the barren, snow-covered plateau. There were, here and there, clumps of trees and bunches of bushes, but not a single house or soul to be seen, only the vast, endless open space. She gave the mule another kick with her heels, forcing it to move faster. Finally, she reached the outskirts of the city. She asked a villager for directions to the military headquarters. After finding out where they were, she moved as fast as she dared through the winding, muddy streets of Skopje.

At the entry to the Ottoman regional military compound, the guard stopped the mule with its human cargo.

"What do you want, woman?" he crudely asked.

Servet, as traditional custom required, covered her face with her wool scarf, and told the guard who she was. She asked him to direct her and her baby to the commanding officer.

The guard insisted on asking Servet to show her identification papers, which he closely examined. At last, the guard asked a passing soldier to take her and the baby to the duty officer's quarters.

The mule plodded wearily to the front of a rundown, wooden building where the duty officer was located. Servet carefully handed the baby to the soldier and then slowly eased off the mule. Taking little Bedia back in her arms, she solemnly entered the building. The soldier opened the door to let her into the duty officer's room. A tall, thin captain with a serious face politely rose to greet her.

As soon as the captain heard of Servet's ordeal, he ordered a cup of hot tea for her. "Madam," he said. "The convoy under the command of Lieutenant Nihad arrived at Skopje just a few hours ago. They were attacked by a group of nationalist soldiers early this morning. With the assistance of reinforcements sent from our regiment, they repelled the attackers, but not without considerable casualties. The survivors are camped at the northwest end of the city."

Servet, concerned about her husband's well-being, anxiously questioned the captain. "What is happening in northern Kosovo?"

"All our military units were ordered to withdraw to the town of Kumanovo in southern Kosovo. During the last few days, there have been attacks on some of our military installations. There was a major cavalry confrontation at the southern end of the Tepe Hills. Fortunately, our cavalry defeated the enemy before they could attack our heavy artillery units withdrawing to Kumanovo. I have no specific information on the whereabouts of your husband. As soon as I receive any information, I'll let you know."

Servet thanked the captain for the information. "Captain," she asked concernedly, "is it possible to send some men to find Jemal, our orderly? He's the one who made it possible for us to get here safely."

Rising from his chair behind the desk, the captain replied, "Madam, he was doing his duty. You're lucky to have been guided by such a devoted and capable soldier. Unfortunately, I cannot spare any of my men at this time to search for only one soldier. I'm sure that such a smart, courageous man will find his way here to Skopje." The captain then ushered Servet out of his room and ordered the guard to take her and Bedia to the family quarters to be settled in.

The other wives in the officers' quarters warmly welcomed Servet and helped settle her into a small room. After cleaning up a bit and feeding the baby, Servet graciously asked one of the young wives to look after Bedia so that she could visit a relative. She hurried out of the building, mounted the mule, and rode toward the northwest end of the town. After a few inquiries, she found the campground where the Yanyevo convoy was located. Most of the carts that had been transporting the wounded soldiers were empty. The whole camp looked deserted. She asked the soldier on guard duty for Lieutenant Nihad. Recognizing Servet, the guard told her that the lieutenant was at the command center in Skopje. She then asked the soldier about the Turkish villagers. He replied that the villagers had settled near a creek on the other side of the hill. Servet urged the mule quickly toward their camp, hoping to find Selim alive and well.

As Servet trotted into the Turkish villagers' campground, the children, recognizing her, ran toward her. They welcomed her with smiles and led her to Selim's tent. The old man was lying on a thick pile of carpets. Two men were sitting on the floor next to him.

Servet walked up next to the old man and whispered, "Selim Baba, how are you?"

Opening his eyes, Selim looked at her with a welcoming smile that brightened his face. "Barely alive, my little daughter," he said.

"I'm just hanging on. I was shot in this morning's attack. I can assure you that I killed at least five of those bastards. I'm so happy that you and your little girl made it to Skopje safely. Jemal did the right thing by leaving the convoy earlier in the morning. The enemy attack was fierce. We lost many people. Reinforcements from Skopje saved us from complete destruction. Is Jemal with you?"

Selim then turned to one of the men next to him and ordered, "Go out and ask him to come in."

Before the man could rise, Servet interrupted, "Jemal isn't here. This morning we were followed by a couple of deserters. He stayed behind in the woods to prevent the vagabonds from harming Bedia and me."

Selim was distressed by this news. He asked Servet to move closer so he could question her. She moved toward him and sat at the edge of the pile of carpets.

"Servet, my dear daughter," Selim said gently. "Tell me in detail where this happened. How long has it been since you left him in the woods?"

Servet provided the old man with details of the events that had occurred at the edge of the forest just a few hours earlier.

Selim was silent for a long moment. He then turned toward the two men next to him. "Get your rifles," he ordered. "Get on your horses and find this remarkable young man. God willing, he'll still be alive. If he is, bring him here. If not, give him a decent burial."

He then turned to Servet. "Do you still have the compass with you?"

She removed the compass from her pocket and handed it to Selim.

As he passed the compass to one of the men, Selim said, "Go with Servet Hanim to the exact location where she entered the city. Head northwest, and stay on mule tracks until you find Jemal. If you notice foot prints on the snow close to the mule tracks, then you know that he is alive and well and has walked to the city. In that case, you may return to the camp. If there are no footprints, go as far as where the plateau meets the forest and search for him around there. Be sure to return before nightfall."

Selim then addressed Servet. "Young lady, get on your mule and show them exactly where you entered the city. Then go home to your baby. Tomorrow, come back to our camp. If it's the will of God, Jemal will be here waiting for you."

In the Valley of Death

Young Avni entered the gorge just as the sun was setting. The eerie spectrum of a violet twilight lingered in the sky above the western ridge. He felt disturbed walking into this valley of death, redolent with the stink of gunpowder and decaying flesh. The scene before him was difficult to comprehend. Dead horses of various shades of black, brown, and white were strewn about at the end of the gorge, bizarrely tangled with the lifeless bodies of men wearing uniforms of various shades of green, gray, and red. He came upon the dead body of his sergeant, lying on his back next to a dead Serbian soldier still clutching his sword. He stood in between the two bodies, imagining the fierceness of the battle that had occurred earlier that day.

He then looked ahead toward the ravine and recognized the corpse of Lieutenant Avni's horse, Yagiz. Jumping over the bodies of several dead soldiers, he reached the lifeless stallion. Standing next to it, he saw the lieutenant beneath the dead stallion. He reached down under the horse's belly to see if the lieutenant was still alive. With a sigh of relief, young Avni felt the lieutenant's chest moving, though barely. "He is alive," he shouted with excitement.

After a long struggle, he was able to pull the lieutenant out from beneath the belly of his faithful steed and lay him gently on his back on the ground. Checking his body carefully for wounds, he found a big gash on the left side of the lieutenant's temple and a deep cut on the right side of his forehead. Young Avni then searched around the battleground to collect overcoats, food, water flasks and ammunition from the corpses. He stored the items next to the lieutenant and moved the unconscious officer to a pile of overcoats he had collected from the battlefield. With water from his canteen, he washed away the blood from the lieutenant's face and carefully cleaned his head wound. Then, cradling the lieutenant's head, he poured a small amount of water into his mouth. Noticing that the lieutenant was now breathing faster and his eyes were rapidly moving beneath his closed eyelids, the young soldier gently lowered the lieutenant's head to the ground. Then he stood up and ran toward the slopes to find the supply carts.

Gathering up a couple of tents, wool blankets, and a few food items, young Avni returned to the spot where he had left the lieutenant. The lieutenant was gone! With relief, he spotted him a few meters ahead, leaning against the solid rock ridge; he was relieving himself.

Limping noticeably, Lieutenant Avni walked back slowly and unsteadily. As he sat on the pile of army coats, he greeted the young soldier and said, "Try pissing with one hand; not so easy! My left arm and shoulder are messed up. My arm might be broken. I feel dizzy and hurt, but I'm glad to be alive. Thanks for taking care of me. How did you find me? What happened this morning?"

"As you ordered, Lieutenant, I reached the commanding officer of the Pristina cavalry. He read your note and then ordered the cavalry regiment to ride to the southern end of the Tepe Hills. I had expected him to send reinforcements to help our unit fight against the approaching enemy. Apparently, he decided to abandon our unit and ordered the cavalry to move toward the southern end of Tepe Hills to face the enemy cavalry. I think such a decision was highly improper. The commander was well aware that without reinforcements the Yanyevo unit would be wiped out, and yet he still ordered me to return to my unit. I just don't understand his reason for such a decision."

Avni leaned against the boulder behind him and said, "I understand his decision perfectly. He chose to surprise the weakened enemy cavalry at the southern end of the valley. Then he decided to send you back here to help the survivors, which you have already done."

After thinking a short while about what Lieutenant Avni had said, young Avni replied, "You're right, Lieutenant. Our cavalry did surprise the enemy at the southern end of the valley, and we destroyed them completely."

"How do you know that?" Lieutenant Avni asked sharply.

"On my way here, I had an unfortunate encounter with a few nationalist soldiers. One of them told me about the defeat of the Serbian cavalry this morning."

Avni was perplexed. "Why on earth did they let you go?" he asked.

The young soldier explained what had happened.

At the mention of Burhan, the lieutenant commented, "Now I know why you're still alive. You're lucky! Did you tell Burhan about his father?"

"Yes, I told him his father was imprisoned in Pristina."

"Did Burhan go back to Pristina?"

"No, he headed north."

"We should go to Pristina to make sure Mehmetali is all right," said Lieutenant Avni. "There is nothing more we can do here for our fallen comrades." Then, rubbing his swollen ankle, he ordered young Avni to check the area before nightfall for other survivors.

"I have already checked. There are no other survivors," young Avni replied.

"I'm sure all the wounded were summarily executed by the enemy before they moved on through the valley," the lieutenant explained.

"I think you were saved from execution because they thought you were already dead," said the young soldier.

"I was lucky to fall under my wounded horse. I thank the Lord for that. Yagiz saved my life. He was a magnificent war horse and a great companion for many months. I'll miss him."

After a long pause, the lieutenant ordered the young soldier to do a few necessary chores. "Before it gets dark," he said, "count the dead in the battle area. It would be great if you could find a medical supply bag and bring it to me."

When it was almost twilight, young Avni returned with a medical bag. The lieutenant asked him to help clean and bandage his head wounds. He then ordered the young soldier to find a few pieces of wood to make a brace of some sort for his broken arm.

As he tightly tied a couple of dried branches to the lieutenant's broken arm, the young soldier informed him of the casualty count. "I'm not sure I took an accurate count in the dimness of twilight," he said. "I think there are two hundred twenty-five dead bodies out in the battle area. Ninety-six of them are ours."

"Discounting the twenty men I assigned to the hills, that leaves twenty-two survivors who escaped execution. Possibly a few of the men up on the hillside escaped death. That means the enemy lost one hundred twenty-nine men, plus the wounded."

Lieutenant Avni raised his good arm and turned his palm toward his face. "Let's pray for our fallen brothers," he said. "Their bravery ensured us a victory today."

Later, after sunset, they ate the food young Avni had collected earlier and made plans for the next day. When total darkness descended on the valley of the dead, they crawled into their tents and slept soundly through the night.

Ceasefire

It was already pitch dark when Burhan and the two nationalist soldiers entered the town of Pudujevo. Burhan was immediately taken to the command center where Karaevitch and several other senior officers were discussing the next day's military strategy. When the meeting ended, Karaevitch dismissed the officers and called Burhan over to him. After Burhan gave him Michailovitch's report, Karaevitch sat down behind his desk and read it.

I agree with Lieutenant Michailovitch, thought the commander. *We should attack in full force and occupy Kosovo completely. With the exception of losing that one cavalry regiment at the southern end of the Tepe Hills, we have hurt the enemy in many parts of Kosovo. The Ottoman army is now withdrawing southward toward Macedonia. More importantly, the Turks and Albanians are leaving Kosovo in droves. Now is the time to make Kosovo ours again. Unfortunately, our beloved King Karageorgevitch, under political pressure from Vienna, has decided against a final push to occupy Kosovo. Our new orders are to withdraw to southern Serbia and cease all hostilities without delay. I'll now write a new set of instructions to Michailovitch.*

Karaevitch turned to Burhan and ordered him to wait outside.

A short while later, the commander came out of his office and handed a sealed envelope to Burhan. "There's no need to attack Pristina," he gruffly said. "Michailovitch should regroup all units around Pristina and Grachanitsa and withdraw to Mitrovica immediately. First thing tomorrow morning, you should deliver these instructions to Lieutenant Michailovitch."

Finishing his meal, Burhan walked out of the warm mess hall into the cold air. The night sky was full of stars. *I should ride through the night and reach Pristina before sunrise,* he thought. *I've to get there before battle-crazed Michailovitch decides to attack the town.*

He waited until after midnight. Before leaving the Serbian military camp in Pudujevo, Burhan told the two soldiers who had traveled with him earlier in the day to report back to their units in Mitrovica. He then got on his black stallion and started the night's journey to Kosovo Polje.

As he rode toward Pristina in the moonlight, he recalled what Rita, the young Gypsy girl, had told him just a few days ago. *Obviously, the Austrians decided to withdraw their soldiers from Kosovo for some political reason,* Burhan thought. *Unfortunately, that decision left the Serbians alone to face a formidable enemy.*

Burhan had seen most of the Ottoman defense preparations during his secret mission. In agreement with the Serbian's decision to pull back to southern Serbia, he muttered to himself, "As both armies are now withdrawing, Kosovo is becoming a no-man's-land."

The Sixteenth of January: Prayers for the Fallen

Lieutenant Avni awoke at dawn, aching in almost every part of his body. Without moving, he recited his morning prayers, thanking the Lord for being alive. He then closed his eyes and prayed a long time for the safety of his family. Completing his prayers, Avni looked out of the tent for young Avni, but he was nowhere to be seen. A short while later, young Avni walked into the lieutenant's tent with a container of water and some old biscuits. He told the lieutenant that he was going to search for a couple of loose horses.

The lieutenant ordered him to sit down. "Young man," he said calmly, "you have no chance of finding any stray horses. The nationalist cavalry has likely taken all the surviving horses with them after yesterday's battle. Listen to me carefully. If we are lucky, the enemy didn't notice the supply animals tethered right above the hidden supply storage along the eastern part of the ridge. Go there and look around. You will, hopefully, find a couple of horses and several mules tied to the trees not far from the storage area. Those two horses are old and slow, but they'll get us to Pristina much faster than the mules. Feed them, make sure they get plenty of water, and then bring them here. Take the saddle from my dead horse. Once both of the horses are saddled, we'll start our journey to Pristina."

An hour later, with the help of young Avni, the lieutenant mounted the old horse. The sun had barely risen, and the hazy morning light slowly illuminated the gruesome remains of the previous day's battle. Lieutenant Avni was silent as he rode the old horse among the bodies of his dead comrades. Turning in his saddle he talked to the young soldier behind him. "Let's pray again for the souls of our fallen brothers," he said. "They gallantly gave their lives for the empire and the faith."

Completing their painful prayers, the two remaining souls of the now-defunct Yanyevo unit began a journey to Pristina to save another soul from possible demise.

Nurjahan in Selim's Camp

Standing outside of Dursun's tent, Nurjahan shouted, "Big brother, wake up! The sun has risen; we must start moving."

Buried under several heavy blankets, Dursun reached out and touched his wife. "We must get to Skopje soon. We are out of food. Please, get up."

As Dursun and his family emerged from their makeshift tent, Nurjahan had both of their horses ready to commence the rest of their journey to Skopje. Dursun helped his wife onto one horse and put his little son on the other, which would be ridden by Nurjahan.

"Thank God," Dursun said as he looked up. "The sky is clear this morning. Now we'll be able to see where we're going."

After a couple of hours, Nurjahan, Dursun, and his family reached the outskirts of Skopje. Spotting a settlement of tents near a creek, Nurjahan suggested to Dursun that they stop and ask for food.

Dursun disagreed. "I don't think we should disturb them."

"We're starving to death and you're worried about disturbing them?" Nurjahan replied sharply. "I'll ask for some bread, if you don't mind."

She stopped her horse, dismounted, and purposefully strode toward one of the tents. Before she could reach it, two husky men came out with their rifles. Pointing their guns at her, they asked in Turkish who she was. Nurjahan told the Turkish villagers where she was from. In return, they told her that they were from a settlement near her village. Following a few more tense but illuminating interactions, Nurjahan, Dursun, and his family were ushered into a warm tent for bread and tea.

As she burst into tears, Nurjahan lamented, "I don't have a village anymore! It was burned to the ground and destroyed." Stepping forward, Dursun recounted the rest of the story to the Turkish villagers.

Soon afterward, their drama was reported to Selim by a village woman while bringing him a cup of tea. Selim, recovering from his bullet wound, attentively listened to the woman telling him the ordeals of Dursun and Nurjahan.

After a few sips of tea, Selim responded, "They are our kin. Such godsend guests should stay as long as they wish." He then asked the woman, "How's Jemal doing? Is he recovering?"

"He's sleeping like a baby. But I think he needs a surgeon to remove the bullet from his shoulder."

"We'll let Servet Hanim arrange the medical attention Jemal needs. Please, let me know as soon as she arrives."

As the village woman was leaving the tent, she asked, "The Albanian man who arrived with the Turkish girl would like to see you to pay his respects."

Selim, feeling tired, closed his eyes. "Not now! I'll see him in due time," he whispered.

Insubordination

Lieutenant Michailovitch ordered the guard to let Burhan enter. "I didn't expect to see you so early," he said to Burhan. "You must have left Pudujevo before dawn." Michailovitch hastily took the envelope from Burhan. As he read the letter from his commanding officer, his face darkened with anger. He cursed loudly, crumpled the letter, and threw it to the floor.

Burhan could guess from the lieutenant's reaction that Michailovitch was not going to obey the orders he had received. It was obvious that there would be no change in the lieutenant's plans; he would proceed with his intention to occupy Pristina and Grachanitsa. Burhan wondered how Commander Karaevitch would react when he found out that his direct orders had been completely disobeyed by Michailovitch.

With a nervous twitch on his lips, Michailovitch spoke. "Burhan, I've been informed that there's a pocket of resistance in Grachanitsa. I'll lead a group of soldiers to eliminate them. At the same time, you should lead an attack on the center of Pristina. Most of the Ottoman army has already withdrawn to southern Kosovo. They've formed new defense lines around Kumanovo. I expect that there'll be little or no resistance in Pristina. When the town is fully occupied, wait for me to raise our flag at the administrative center. You should get your men ready for action; we move in two hours."

Alive and Well

Before leaving the room, Servet wrapped Bedia in thick blankets. She climbed onto her mule, and a young woman handed up her baby. Anxious to reach the Turkish villagers' camp to find Jemal, she kicked the sides of the mule with her heels and murmured, "I pray to the Lord Almighty that Jemal is alive and well." The day before, she had taken two of Selim's men to the edge of the city and watched them ride across the snow-covered plains in search of Jemal.

When Servet entered the tent, Selim was talking to Dursun. She greeted both men and sat down on a pile of soft carpets. Holding her precious baby close to her bosom, she listened intently to the conversation between the two men. Dursun was describing in detail the fate of his now-destroyed village. He described how they had been saved by an Albanian serving in the Serbian nationalist force. Dursun concluded his story with the description of how they had escaped the carnage, and finally reached Macedonia. He thanked the old man for his generosity in providing shelter and food to his family.

Selim, lying on his side, cleared his throat. "My dear Albanian brother, I know your village well. I've been there on many occasions for weddings, funerals, and other celebrations. I remember the natural beauty of your village. Most importantly, I'll never forget that, as brothers of the faith, we coexisted in peace and harmony. I'm very sorry to hear about its destruction. May the good Lord grant eternal peace to the departed souls of your village and provide you with the courage and stamina to build a new life for yourself and your family. What are your plans, my young brother?"

Dursun, eyes downcast, spoke almost in a whisper. "We'll move to Anatolia, where, God willing, a secure and prosperous life awaits us."

"A very good decision, indeed," Selim said. "Until you make your travel arrangements to Anatolia, you are most welcome to stay with us. What are your plans for the young Turkish girl you have with you?"

"She also would like to come with us to Anatolia," Dursun replied. He then asked, "Selim Efendi, what are you and the village folks planning to do? Are you thinking of going back to your village?"

"Yes, God willing, we'd like to return. But until that is possible, we'll wait in a safe corner of Macedonia."

Dursun, before rising, took the venerable old man's hand in his own. Showing the ultimate sign of respect, he kissed the back of the old man's hand and touched it briefly to his own forehead.

After Dursun had departed, Selim motioned Servet closer. "My young daughter, have you seen Jemal yet?"

"Yes, I saw him just before I came into your tent. I'd like to take him to the military hospital. Could someone help me get him to the city?"

"Of course, we'll do whatever we can for you! I presume you came here with your mule. We'll harness a cart to your mule. While one of our boys rides the animal, you and your baby girl can sit with Jemal in the cart."

Servet thanked the old man. "Selim Baba, Jemal wasn't able to say much. Do you know what happened during his rescue?"

"Yes, I know," replied Selim. "I was told by the men who brought him here late last night. He was found exactly where you left him yesterday morning, lying on the snow-covered ground near the cart. His feet and hands were tied. His overcoat, jacket, and shoes were gone. He had a bullet wound in the upper part of his left shoulder and a gash on the right side of his head. When our men found him, he was half conscious. If my men had not reached him by nightfall, he would have died from exposure. Jemal told me that it was a couple of Ottoman army deserters who shot him, took his clothes, and left him to die in the snow. You know, Servet Hanim, he saved the lives of both you and your daughter. In return, you saved his life. Let's thank the Lord for making this possible."

Servet replied gratefully, "And you, my dear Baba, saved all our lives. God bless and protect you and your loved ones."

As she rose to leave the tent, Selim pleaded with her. "Please talk to Lieutenant Nihad. Convince him not take disciplinary action against Jemal for abandoning the convoy."

An hour later, a couple of young boys from the camp harnessed the mule and attached it to a cart. The two men who had rescued Jemal from the wilderness the previous evening carried him out on a wooden stretcher and carefully laid him down inside the cart. Servet thanked both men profusely for their efforts to save Jemal's life. She then got into the cart with her baby and sat next to Jemal.

"This dreadful journey has ended well for the three of us," she said. "If it's the will of God, my husband will also join us, alive and well, in Skopje."

A Sitting Duck

It would have been another uneventful day for Mehmetali if the guards had brought his usual morning meal on time. When he looked from the tiny window of the cell door, there was no one in sight. The eerie quietness in the hallways of the jailhouse disturbed Mehmetali.

He shouted, "Where is everybody?"

There was no answer, only silence. He turned away from the door and walked to the window to have a look at the back of the building. There was no one in the alley, not a single soul. He ran back to the door, shouting the names of the guards several times. No one responded to his frustrated pleas.

Mehmetali remembered being told by a guard that the last prisoner had been executed three days earlier. He and the three guards were the only ones who remained in the special interrogation holding unit. Apparently, he was the only one left on the whole floor. A few days ago, he had been informed by one of the guards that everyone in the city would soon be evacuated. With the exception of a few soldiers, everyone was scheduled to leave Pristina. When Mehmetali asked when he would be released, the guard replied that he had not yet received an order from his superiors to let him go, and that was that. So it looked as if he had been left behind in a locked cell and had become a sitting duck for the arriving Serbian soldiers. He cursed his rotten luck. Taking the last cigarette out of his pocket, he decided to enjoy a few moments of pleasure before the Serbians' arrival.

The Rescue

Lieutenant Avni stopped directly in front of the building where Mehmetali was supposed to be jailed and dismounted from the old horse with the help of young Avni. Once he set foot on the ground, Lieutenant Avni advised the young soldier to scout the dining hall for some food.

"Lieutenant," young Avni asked before departing, "do you really think anyone still is here? I think Mehmetali is on his way to Yanyevo or Skopje. We're wasting our time here. We should get out before the Serbian soldiers take over the city."

The lieutenant looked at him sternly. "Young man," he snapped. "There is no need for insubordination. Do what I told you. While you search for food, I'll look inside the building to make sure Mehmetali is gone. We'll leave as soon as you return with something to eat."

Expecting that at least a few guards or soldiers would have stayed behind, Lieutenant Avni cautiously entered the building. There was no one at the guard station. He passed through the guards' room and entered the long hallway with four cells on each side. All he could hear was the barking of a dog outside. As he was about to turn around and retrace his steps out of the building, he suddenly heard a deep cough peculiar to heavy smokers coming from one of the cells on the left side of the hallway. Striding toward the cell door, Avni shouted Mehmetali's name. He stopped in front of the heavy iron door and pressed his face onto the small window to see who was inside the cell. He saw the bearded face of his old friend staring at him in disbelief.

Mehmetali cried, "Lieutenant, what a pleasant surprise! I was expecting the bloody Serbian executioners! It's so good to see you."

Avni's ear-to-ear grin showed how happy he was to see his old friend. "Hold on, I'll find the keys and let you out."

Avni returned to the guards' room to find the keys to the cells. As he was searching for the keys, young Avni entered the room in a hurry. "The Serbian soldiers are about to enter the city!" he shouted. "We must leave now, Lieutenant."

"First we've got to find the keys to Mehmetali's cell," Lieutenant Avni replied.

"You found Mehmetali?" young Avni asked excitedly. "He's still here? Is he all right?"

"Yes, he's fine, but he's locked in a cell. We have to find the keys."

Drawing his pistol, young Avni suggested shooting the lock off the cell door.

The lieutenant grabbed the young soldier's arm. "You just told me that the Serbians are about to enter the town," he said gruffly. "And now you want to use your gun to open the cell door. Do you think that is a smart thing to do? We must find the keys."

Lieutenant Avni ran to the main operations building, desperately hoping to find someone who knew where the guards had gone. Before he could reach the adjacent brick building, he heard gunshots nearby. Realizing that the enemy soldiers were very close, he quickly returned to the guards' room and ordered young Avni to go outside and bring his rifle. When young Avni again suggested using his own pistol, the lieutenant told him that with a rifle he might be able to break the lock with a single shot.

After young Avni shot and broke the lock to the iron door, Mehmetali walked out of the jail cell with a big grin on his face and embraced the lieutenant. Noticing the wrapped white bandage on his head and the wooden braces on his arm, Mehmetali said, "You look as if you have been through hell."

Lieutenant Avni, still smiling, replied, "You guessed right. I have been through hell and more. I'll tell you all about it."

Young Avni impatiently interrupted to inform them that the nationalist soldiers were approaching. "We should leave the town quickly," he said. "Otherwise, we'll be trapped when the Serbians surround this building."

They ran out of the building and had almost reached their horses when several rifle shots were fired. A bullet hit Lieutenant Avni in the upper part of his right leg. While young Avni crouched to shoot at a group of Serbian soldiers across the street, Mehmetali helped the lieutenant retreat into the building. Young Avni followed them in and slammed the heavy wooden door behind them.

"Lieutenant, are you all right?" asked the young soldier.

Lieutenant Avni, staring at his bloody leg, replied, "It doesn't look good. We have to stop the bleeding." Mehmetali rushed in from the guards' room with a first-aid kit. As he prepared to apply a pressure bandage to the lieutenant's leg wound, Mehmetali told the young soldier to keep an eye on the Serbian soldiers. While wrapping the last roll of gauze tightly around the wounded leg, Mehmetali realized no shots had been fired since they had re-entered the building. He looked at young Avni who was leaning against the slightly ajar wooden door, rifle on shoulder, sweeping for a target. "What do you see out there?" he asked.

Without changing his position, young Avni replied, "Nothing! No one is around! This is very strange. They stopped shooting at us. I wonder why?"

Searching for Father

After saluting Burhan, one Serbian soldier asked if they should continue attacking the building where a couple of Ottoman soldiers were hiding. As he dismounted, Burhan looked at the building across the street. "Not yet!" he replied. "We have to make sure that there are no nationalist prisoners in there before we attack. Leave three soldiers with me. Take the rest of the company with you to clear out the administration building. Make sure it's completely secured before Lieutenant Michailovitch appears in Pristina. I'll handle the Ottoman soldiers in the building."

Burhan ordered the three soldiers to follow him across the street. They carefully approached the prison and took cover behind a large tree near the building. Burhan, facing the entry door, shouted in Turkish, "I'll negotiate your surrender with your leader. We'll not shoot unless you force us. What do you say?" There was no answer, so he repeated the message.

A few minutes later, he heard his father's voice. "We're ready to negotiate. Come in unarmed and we'll talk." Handing over his rifle, Burhan ordered the soldiers to stay in their positions until he returned. With cautious, measured steps, he walked toward the prison building.

Young Avni opened the door to let Burhan enter. Recognizing the young soldier, Burhan smiled. "I didn't expect to see you again," he said gleefully. "I left you in the middle of nowhere and you've survived without a horse. Why are you here?"

Burhan did not wait for an answer; he saw his father walking toward him. He was glad to see him alive. He then noticed Lieutenant Avni lying on the floor a few meters away. After giving his father a warm hug, Burhan asked, "Is the lieutenant badly wounded?"

"God willing, son, he'll survive," Mehmetali replied. "How did you know I was here?"

With a smiling glance at young Avni, who was standing next to the door, Burhan replied, "It appears that by mere luck all of us here knew where you were. Actually, it was the lieutenant who made it possible for us to meet. Anyway, we now have to decide quickly what to do next."

A few minutes later, Burhan left the building. The three Serbian soldiers were still waiting for him behind cover. He told them that the Ottoman soldiers had decided to surrender if their lives could be spared. Burhan ordered the soldiers to follow him into the prison building. To assure them that they would not be ambushed, he said, "I've taken their guns away and locked them in a cell."

When the Serbian soldiers entered the building, young Avni and Mehmetali pointed their guns at their heads. Even the lieutenant, lying wounded on the floor, had a revolver pointed at them. One by one, the nationalist soldiers were forced to take off their uniforms. They were then gagged, bound, and locked into separate cells. After changing into Serbian uniforms, Mehmetali and young Avni helped the lieutenant into a nationalist soldier's uniform. Burhan advised them to take the Ottoman uniforms with them to change back into later.

Realizing that there was not an extra uniform for Burhan, Mehmetali said, "We must find an Ottoman uniform for you, or at least an overcoat."

"Father," Burhan said hurriedly. "Don't worry about it. Before it's too late, you've got to get away. I'll help Lieutenant Avni. Both of you go and get the horses ready." He then turned to the lieutenant and asked, "Can you stand up?"

"Yes, but on one foot only," replied Avni. "I don't think I can walk by myself."

"Lean on my shoulder," said Burhan. "We'll walk out together. I hope you can ride?"

With a painful smile, Avni replied, "I think I'll be fine on a horse."

Standing at the doorway, young Avni shouted, "The horses are ready. But we have only two; we need three horses."

"You ride one, and let my father and the lieutenant ride the other," ordered Burhan.

"What about you?" asked young Avni.

"I've got to remain behind. I'll meet you in Yanyevo tomorrow. Hide in the woods until sunset. Then move southeast during the night. Do not use the main roads. If I don't show up by tomorrow evening, you start your journey to Skopje the following day. When you get close to Kumanovo, change into Ottoman uniforms."

Helping his father onto the horse behind Lieutenant Avni, Burhan clasped his father's hand. "Have a safe trip," he said. "God willing, I'll see you tomorrow in Yanyevo."

"Son," Mehmetali said. "It'll warm my heart to welcome you home."

Serbian Flag in Pristina

Lieutenant Michailovitch, riding high and proud on his horse, entered Pristina. He stopped in front of the main administration building. As he dismounted, he asked the sergeant, "Did you face any resistance? Any casualties?"

"We have no casualties, sir. However, Burhan and the three soldiers he took with him have been missing for the last couple of hours."

"Why did he separate from his unit?"

"I don't know, Lieutenant. All I know is that his unit secured this area and several Ottoman government buildings a few hours ago. Do you want me to investigate?"

"No need for investigation, Sergeant. I can see Burhan at the far end of the field among some soldiers. Tell him to come here."

As he slowly walked toward the lieutenant, Burhan could see the Serbian nationalist flag being raised in the distance. He was prepared to depart Pristina once and for all, definitely before the half-naked gagged soldiers in the cells were discovered. But he first wanted to know the lieutenant's immediate plans for the next few days. Only then would he permanently leave his unit and return home.

Approaching Michailovitch, Burhan saluted him. "Greetings, Lieutenant," he said impassively.

"You have done a good job, Burhan. Now we're flying our flag on the old Serbian soil. We haven't conquered all of it yet, but soon we'll accomplish that too. How was your entry to Pristina this morning? Any problems?"

"No problems at all, Lieutenant. We took over the town without any incident. There was no resistance, except for a couple of guards in the prison. We took care of them."

"I've been informed that you're missing three men," inquired Michailovitch.

"No, Lieutenant, they're not missing. They are presently on guard duty. What are your plans for tomorrow?"

"I haven't decided yet," replied Michailovitch. "We'll talk about it later this afternoon."

Burhan casually walked away from the lieutenant toward his men hanging around the flag post. He told one of the soldiers to follow him to the prison building. Stopping in front of the prison, he ordered the soldier to guard the building and not to let anyone inside under any circumstances.

On the Way to Yanyevo

Lieutenant Avni was in great pain. He remembered Burhan's suggestion to travel only during the night. "Mehmetali," he said. "I think we've traveled far enough into the woods. Let's stop here. We'll continue after sunset."

Mehmetali shouted to young Avni to stop. As he dismounted from the horse, he asked, "How is your leg, Lieutenant?"

"I'm all right, Mehmetali. I just need some rest."

"I think you need serious medical attention, Lieutenant. You have a head wound, a broken arm, and a bullet in your thigh. Doctor Nuri will be busy putting you back together."

"Do you think Doctor Nuri will still be in Yanyevo?" Lieutenant Avni asked.

"I really don't know; I presume so," replied Mehmetali.

"I'd be surprised if any medical personnel still remain in Yanyevo. We'll find out tomorrow, won't we? Now I need to rest."

Mehmetali and young Avni helped the lieutenant dismount and lie on a blanket on the ground. As raindrops began to spatter on his balding head, Mehmetali asked young Avni to erect a temporary shelter over the lieutenant.

Huddling closely, the three men listened to large rain drops monotonously hit the canvas cover over their heads. When the rain stopped, they spoke about the Yanyevo troops' unfortunate battle. Mehmetali was sad to hear of the loss of so many of his friends from the Yanyevo unit. He remarked that the victory for the Ottoman cavalry had been possible through the intelligent and strategic decisions taken by the lieutenant and, of course, by the heroic sacrifices of the Yanyevo troops.

Lieutenant Avni described the final moments of the battle when his horse, Yagiz, had collapsed over him, knocking him out cold.

Tears in his eyes, Mehmetali whispered, "I loved that horse. Even in death, the brave horse provided cover for your survival, Lieutenant."

Later, young Avni spoke about what Burhan had unexpectedly done when he and his soldiers caught up with him as he was riding back to Tepe Hills. Mehmetali had a big smile on his face. He was visibly proud of his son's good intentions and quick thinking. They kept talking until dusk. After dark, they mounted and rode slowly and silently toward Yanyevo.

Young Avni asked the lieutenant if they should change into their Ottoman uniforms.

"No, not yet," the lieutenant answered. "We are still traveling through enemy territory."

The End of Michailovitch

During the staff meeting early that evening, Burhan sat close to Lieutenant Michailovitch. As usual, the lieutenant was boasting loudly about the day's victory. "To complete our victory tomorrow, we'll move east and occupy the few towns that remain in the hands of those damned Turks. Kosovo will be ours again. Now let's celebrate what we accomplished today." He turned to one of the soldiers standing nearby and ordered drinks for everyone.

Burhan's instincts told him that it was time to move out and get on the road to Yanyevo. He stood up to leave.

"Where are you going, my friend?" shouted Michailovitch.

Burhan replied over his shoulder. "Nature calls, Lieutenant."

"Come back quickly. I need to talk to you."

Burhan quickly left the meeting room and rushed to the prison to check on the guard posted in front of the building. The soldier was standing still near the door. Without being asked he said, "No one has come, Sergeant."

"Very well! Remain here until the relief guard comes in two hours," Burhan ordered. Then he went behind the building to check on his horse. He made sure he had the proper equipment and supplies for the long journey ahead. After a thorough inspection of the supplies, he was confident that he was ready to travel. As he strolled back to the main hall where Michailovitch was waiting for him, Burhan wondered how Commander Karaevitch would react when he discovered that Lieutenant Michailovitch had disobeyed a direct order and proceeded with attacks on Pristina and Grachanitsa. Knowing both officers' temperaments, Burhan was sure that such blatant insubordination would end with Michailovitch's arrest and court martial.

After Burhan had taken his seat at the table, Michailovitch bellowed at him, "You, my friend, have witnessed the end of the sinking Ottoman Empire. Today was the beginning of the end. We finally have arrived at Kosovo Polje, our true home."

Burhan could not agree more with the lieutenant. He was well aware that the Ottoman occupation of Eastern Europe had been solidified with the victory at Kosovo Polje more than five hundred years ago. *But today,* he thought, *the Ottoman Army's retreat from the symbolic site had possibly signaled the end of the Turkish presence in Europe.* He did not, however, agree with the lieutenant's assumption that Kosovo Polje had retained its Serbian identity after more than half a millennium of Ottoman rule. *Michailovitch is damn wrong,* Burhan mused. *The Kosovo of today is more Albanian than Serbian.*

During the rest of the evening, Michailovitch kept drinking heavily, giving orders left and right to everyone in the room. He ordered Burhan to take charge of cleaning out the few remaining towns in the hands of the Ottomans in southern parts of Kosovo. Burhan appeared attentive, but knew that he would perform no more tasks for the Serbian nationalist cause. In his opinion, the time was ripe for an Albanian rebellion in the Balkans to retain areas that were ethnically and culturally Albanian.

Burhan was suddenly startled from his reflections on the possibility of an Albanian state by loud noises coming from the entrance to the administrative building. The door to the meeting room burst open, followed by an onrush of well-armed Serbian soldiers grouped around an officer. The stocky Serbian officer, a captain, strode toward Lieutenant Michailovitch, who had been shocked into silence by their forceful entry. With his right hand resting lightly on a revolver that was hooked onto his wide army belt, the surly-looking captain handed an envelope to Michailovitch, and, in a strong and authoritative voice, proclaimed, "Lieutenant Michailovitch, you are relieved of your command. You are under arrest. Come with me."

Michailovitch made a sudden move toward his gun. Two guards next to the captain quickly aimed their rifles at his head. The captain ordered Michailovitch to hand over his revolver. He then announced that all military activities were to cease and the nationalist forces were to withdraw back to the Serbian border.

Burhan, a broad smile on his sunburned face, realized that, as of tomorrow, Kosovo Polje would again belong to the Ottomans, perhaps only temporarily, until competitive political forces in London, Paris, Vienna, Moscow, and Belgrade could work out an agreement to divide the spoils of the declining Ottoman Empire. He felt that this political stalemate would be a lucky break for Albanian independence advocates such as Ismail Kemal Vlora and Hasan Bey Berisha. He was greatly relieved to see Michailovitch, his longtime Serbian comrade-in-arms, marched away in manacles. Now he was ready to walk away from it all. He stood up and quietly stepped out of the meeting hall.

When he reached the prison building, he ordered the guard to go inside and release the three Serbian soldiers locked in the cells. He then hurriedly walked to the back of the prison building, mounted his horse, and swiftly rode into the dark forest. After a few kilometers of galloping, he slowed down the horse. He was finally on his way home.

The Seventeenth of January: Yanyevo Liberated

In the dark of the night, Lieutenant Avni saw the twinkling lights of Yanyevo in the distance. "We're about to reach our destination," he told his comrades. "I suggest we stop to discuss a strategy for entering the town safely. We should be very careful entering Yanyevo. We don't know who now controls the town. I think one of us should go into town wearing civilian clothes."

"I could do that," said Mehmetali. "I'm the only one with civilian clothes in my saddlebag."

Before departing, Mehmetali approached Lieutenant Avni. "Lieutenant," he said. "If I don't come back, you should continue traveling to Skopje."

"I don't think I'm strong enough to make it to Skopje," replied Avni. "Besides, we don't have the equipment or supplies for three full days of travel. Go ahead, proceed and assess the situation. If there's any danger, you'll let us know. We'll wait for you here. If you don't return within the next four hours, we'll proceed to Colonel Husnu's house. God protect you!"

At the outskirts of Yanyevo, Mehmetali dismounted his horse, tied the reins to a tree, and walked into town, staying on the dark and shadowy sides of the narrow, twisting side streets. It was after midnight. The town was asleep. He decided to first check Colonel Husnu's house to see if he was still in command. In front of the colonel's house, Mehmetali spotted three horses with their reins tied to a tree. Like a ghost, he moved silently toward the horses. The look of the saddles and the harnesses revealed to Mehmetali that these horses belonged to Serbian nationalist soldiers. He quietly withdrew from the area and decided to visit the house of one of his closest relatives for more information.

After a long discussion with one of his sisters-in-law, Mehmetali discovered that the town had been attacked by a small band of nationalist soldiers a few days earlier. The colonel and Doctor Nuri had been killed. The few remaining soldiers and hospital staff had either been killed or had escaped into the woods. All the nationalist soldiers, except the three now staying in the colonel's house, had left Yanyevo the previous day.

Mehmetali rushed back into the forest. He explained to Lieutenant Avni in detail the dangerous situation prevailing in Yanyevo. "Lieutenant, what do you suggest we do now?" he asked.

They sat together on the ground, discussing their options in the dark. One hour later, they mounted their horses and rode into town. Arriving at Yanyevo before dawn, Mehmetali and young Avni dismounted. They helped the lieutenant dismount and positioned him next to a large tree trunk across from the door of the colonel's house. Lieutenant Avni sat on the ground and placed his revolver near his good arm. He then asked young Avni to hand him a rifle. As he propped the rifle on a large boulder in front of him, he took aim with one arm at the door of the house. "This is a good range," he said with confidence. "I'll shoot them dead as they come out. You two get into position. Right at sunrise, when we have enough light to pick and choose, you two enter the house with the intention of killing the bastards. If any one of them manages to get out of the house alive, they'll face my rifle."

Mehmetali acknowledged Lieutenant Avni's instructions. "This is a very good plan, Lieutenant. We'll kill these Serbian bastards and liberate the town." Mehmetali and the young soldier sat on the ground next to the lieutenant and quietly waited for dawn.

Homecoming

Burhan sighted the outskirts of Yanyevo before dawn. He decided to wait for sunrise before entering the town. He erected his tent in a wooded area in the hills. After eating a piece of dry bread and a chunk of cheese he had pocketed during the previous night's dinner, he lay down to rest. A short while later, he awoke to the sound of gunshots from the center of town. He immediately started to pack his gear.

By the time he finished packing, the town was again immersed in silence. As he sat on his gear pack, he felt the misty morning air on his face and wondered about the gunshots. He hoped his father and his companions were all right. He mounted his horse and, as he was riding, took his rifle from the sheath on the saddle, making sure that it was fully loaded. He slung the rifle over his right shoulder. His mind was puzzled about the source of the early-morning clash. He dug his heels into the sides of his horse, urging the animal to move faster.

When he arrived at Yanyevo less than an hour later, he came upon a crowd of people gathered around the coffeehouse across from the mosque. Recognizing his nationalist uniform, everyone scattered. Burhan realized that he should have taken off his uniform before entering the town. He quickly got his rifle ready and prepared to fire in self-defense. Suddenly he heard the sharp crackle of a single-load rifle being cocked into firing position, and felt the bullet pass just above his ear. He threw himself off the horse. From his position on the ground, he raised his rifle up toward the sky and raised his other hand, fingers outstretched, in the direction of the gunshot. In a loud voice, Burhan identified himself and announced that he was in town to look for his father. He repeated the message several times. No shots were fired. He slowly put his rifle on the ground and stood up. Keeping his hands up, he walked toward the nearby building.

Two old local Albanian men, whom he recognized, cautiously approached Burhan with rifles aimed at his head. One of the men recognized him, called his name, and asked him why he was there. Burhan repeated that his father and Lieutenant Avni were supposed to meet him in Yanyevo. The men lowered their guns and told Burhan to follow them to the hospital. At the hospital building, Burhan was ushered into a room where he found Lieutenant Avni lying on a makeshift bed. Next to him a nurse was tending his wounds.

"Burhan, you're here," whispered Avni. "I'm so glad to see you. Come closer. We have to talk."

As he pulled a chair up next to the bed, Burhan asked, "This morning I heard gunshots. What happened?"

"At dawn, we attacked and killed the three nationalist soldiers remaining in Yanyevo. During the fight, young Avni received a deep knife wound in his arm. He is hurt, but he'll recover."

Lieutenant Avni paused to retain his composure. "I'm sorry to tell you that during the skirmish with the Serbian soldiers, your father was badly wounded. While he was fighting hand-to-hand with a nationalist soldier, he was shot from behind." Turning toward the nurse, Avni continued, "This is Fatma. She doesn't think your father will survive the night. She'll take you to him. Go and be with your father now. Later we'll talk more."

As he hurriedly departed the lieutenant's room, Burhan found young Avni in the hallway waiting for him. His right arm was completely wrapped with gauze full of fresh blood stains. The knife wound in the upper part of his arm was still bleeding.

Young Avni, clearly upset, had tears in his eyes. "Burhan," he said. "I'm really sorry about your father. We assumed the third man would try to escape when we attacked the other two soldiers. Mehmetali, after quietly finishing off one soldier with his knife, was about to leave through the bedroom window. That was when he was shot from behind by the third Serbian soldier who had rushed in from the adjacent room. The bastard was shot dead by the lieutenant as he tried to leave the house. At the same time, in the next room, I was fighting hand-to-hand with another Serbian soldier. The bastard was huge, but I won."

Burhan warmly held the young soldier's left shoulder. "You've done a good job, young man," he said. "Now I must see my father. I'll talk to you later."

Nurse Fatma led Burhan into a darkened room where Mehmetali lay motionless on a bed. The nurse informed him that she had been able to stop the external bleeding of the wound in his father's back, but could not stop the internal bleeding in his right lung. "All the doctors are dead," she said. "Our equipment and supplies were destroyed by the nationalists three days ago, when they attacked the town. If this hospital were fully operational, we could save your father's life, but as it is, there isn't much we can do for him. He has only a few hours to live. I'm very sorry."

Burhan sat quietly next to his father, holding his hand for a long time. As the tears rolled down his cheeks, he prayed for a miracle to keep his father alive.

"My son, you're home," Mehmetali whispered. "I'm so happy to see you. Don't be sad, my son. I know my time is up. Yours is just starting. I have a few requests to make of you, son. Please bury me next to your mother and your brother. I've heard the head nurse say that Lieutenant Avni will need serious medical attention very soon. Otherwise, he'll also join me in my final journey to meet the Lord. Take Lieutenant Avni to Skopje as soon as you can. Do it before it is too late. He's a good man. God willing, he'll meet his newborn child. You're the only one who can do that for him."

Clutching his father's hand, Burhan responded, "Your requests shall be fulfilled, Father. I'll see to it. The lieutenant will survive and be with his family soon." Burhan then told his father what happened in Pristina after they had left the day before. They laughed when Burhan described the arrest of Michailovitch. He also told his father about his dream of an independent Albania, and about the possibility of that dream coming true one day.

Sad News for Servet

Servet, walking with pride and poise, entered Lieutenant Nihad's office. Nihad stood to welcome her.

"It's nice to see you, madam. How's your little girl?" he asked.

"She's very well, thank you," replied Servet.

After serving her a cup of tea, Lieutenant Nihad sat behind his desk. "Madam," he said. "I've heard that you saved Jemal's life. What you did was very heroic."

"Thank you, Lieutenant. Compared to what Jemal did for me and for my child, my little effort to help him to safety is nothing. However, I do want to take this opportunity to ask if you've decided not to take disciplinary action against Jemal for leaving the camp without your permission."

"I've given a lot of thought to what happened, but I haven't yet decided what action I'll take to discipline Jemal. However, this meeting is not about him; it's about you. I've received news from the front about Lieutenant Avni. A few survivors of his unit reported that the lieutenant put up a heroic defense at the northern part of Tepe Hills against a formidable enemy cavalry unit. Their sacrifice resulted in a major victory for us later in the day at the southern end of the hills, but I am very sorry to inform you that the survivors also reported that your husband died while fighting the enemy. I have been asked by the general's office to convey our deepest sympathies and condolences. Your husband died fighting for his sovereign and his faith. May the Lord grant him eternal peace in heaven."

Servet, tears coursing down her cheeks, stood up and walked out of Nihad's office without a word. Once outside the office building, she stood motionless in the grass, trying hard to retain her composure. Covering her face with her scarf to hide her tears, she gracefully walked to the residential compound. Entering her room, she gently asked the young girl looking after Bedia to leave. Rocking the baby snugly in her arms, she wept silently.

The Eighteenth of January: Bruised Souls

Almost everybody in the small town of Yanyevo attended the early-morning burial ceremony of Mehmetali, who had passed away in his son's arms during the night. Both Lieutenant Avni and young

Avni stood next to Burhan during the final prayers for the soul of the departed.

After the funeral, as she cleaned Avni's wounds, Nurse Fatma told Burhan that if he was to survive, the lieutenant should receive immediate medical attention for his leg wound. She was afraid that the wound would soon become gangrenous. Burhan abruptly left the treatment room to get the horses and supplies ready to take Lieutenant Avni to Skopje. Within a couple of hours, Avni and Burhan were ready to leave Yanyevo. Nurse Fatma and young Avni helped the lieutenant mount his horse. They stood on the stairs of the hospital building to bid farewell to Burhan and the lieutenant. Lieutenant Avni, trying not to show his pain, gratefully asked Fatma to come closer to him. "I wholeheartedly agree with my wife's choice of the name Fatma for our daughter," he said. "We'll always remember you affectionately. May the Lord protect you and your family, and grant you a healthy, long life full of happiness."

Avni then saluted the young soldier who was trying hard to hide his tears. "Young man," he said. "You are a true hero. You've risked your life to save mine. I'll recommend that the high command recognize your heroic activities, which contributed greatly to our recent victory at the Tepe Hills. God bless you!"

In less than an hour, they reached the high ground overlooking the town. Avni asked Burhan to stop his horse and look back. "Barely two weeks ago, in this exact spot," he reminisced, "I looked back at Yanyevo and wondered if I would ever see it again. Now, here I am, one of the few who survived the journey to the battle-ground in Tepe Hills. May the Lord grant a place in heaven to those who lost their lives. I'll truly miss your father, Burhan. He was a loyal and caring friend."

Burhan thanked the lieutenant for the genuine care and sincere attention he had given to his father. "I'll also miss him a lot," he said sorrowfully. "He was a loving husband and caring father."

"Of course he was," Avni said. "I am sure you realize that your father would have been proud and happy to see you in the uniform you're wearing now. You look good in Ottoman colors."

They continued their journey to Skopje without incident. Riding serenely, they talked about many different things, including Burhan's reasons for joining the nationalists, the future of Albanians, and the lurking dangers for the empire of the Turks. When they camped for the night, Burhan fixed a delicious Albanian meal over the bonfire.

"You're a good cook, Burhan, like your father," Avni commented.

"Thank you, Lieutenant. I'm glad to see that you have a good appetite. Soon, you'll recover from your wounds."

"And if it is God's will," Avni said, "tomorrow I'll be united with my wife and meet my daughter."

It was a cold, clear, and star-studded evening. Conversing into the late hours of the night, they told each other many captivating stories. During their slumber, a gentle wind wafted over the tents like a lullaby soothing the bruised but recovering souls of the two remarkable young men.

The Nineteenth of January: Father and Daughter

In the early hours of the next evening, Avni and Burhan reached Skopje. Burhan asked a soldier on the street for directions to the military hospital. Once there, he assisted the medics in carrying Avni into the emergency room. After a preliminary treatment, Avni was put in a large room with many beds filled with wounded officers. He asked Burhan to sit next to the bed so they could talk until the nurse came to prepare him for the operation.

"What are you planning to do next, Burhan?"

"I think I'll go back to Yanyevo tomorrow. Even though I no longer have any family there, it's still home." Burhan paused briefly; then he put his hand on Avni's arm. "Lieutenant," he said. "It was a great honor to get to know you. I told the guards outside to inform your family of your arrival. Soon, your wife and child will arrive to greet you."

Just as Burhan completed his sentence, Servet, clutching Bedia in her arms, rushed into the room. Burhan stood up and gave his seat to her. As he left the ward, Burhan glanced back at the emotional reunion of Lieutenant Avni and his family. He silently walked out of the hospital into the muddy streets of Skopje to find a place to sleep for the night.

Avni held his little daughter in his arms for a long time. Servet, wiping the tears off her cheeks, reached out for Avni's hand. "Yesterday morning," she murmured, "they told me that you were dead. I cried all night. It's a miracle that you survived the battle. Everyone thought you were dead. Tell me what happened."

Avni told her the whole story. Servet was greatly saddened by the death of Mehmetali. "It was his son who brought you here. Isn't he the one who joined the enemy army?" she asked.

"Yes, indeed, he's the one," replied Avni. "Now he's back on his home turf. In a rather strange way, he has served his country very well indeed."

Because Servet was not yet informed of the deaths of Colonel Husnu and Doctor Nuri, Avni decided not to mention the vicious nationalist attack on Yanyevo right before the cease-fire.

It was now Servet's turn to tell her story. She told Avni about the birth of their daughter Bedia and the treacherous journey to Skopje. Servet then informed Avni about Jemal's decision to leave the convoy before it was attacked by the nationalist irregular soldiers. She requested that Avni speak with

Lieutenant Nihad and encourage him not to take disciplinary action against Jemal.

"I'll talk to Nihad when I see him. God bless Jemal. I'd like to see him soon."

Tears pouring down her face, Servet replied, "He'd be very happy to see you, too."

"Why are you crying then?" Avni asked.

She looked into her husband's dark brown eyes. "You were presumed dead," she whispered. "I'm just overwhelmed with your return to my life. My dear husband, these are tears of joy and happiness."

The Twentieth of January: A Tragic Encounter

The next morning, the first thing Lieutenant Nihad did was visit Avni. Unfortunately, Nihad was not able to see him because when Nihad arrived at the hospital, Avni was in surgery. He was asked to visit later in the afternoon. He left the hospital and decided to walk back to his office through the main market. He strolled through the crowded, busy streets and stopped by a coffeehouse for a cup of tea. He sat at a corner table facing the door. He was feeling good about Avni's survival.

The wooden door of the coffeehouse was suddenly flung open with a loud clatter. Two young men entered. One was wearing a soldier's uniform and the other was in civilian clothes. Lieutenant Nihad, recognizing the one in uniform, muttered to himself, "I know this man. He is Burhan, Mehmetali's son. He is a traitor!" He removed his gun from the holster and strode toward the two men who had taken a table nearby. He pointed the gun at Burhan's face and shouted, "You are the son of Mehmetali from Yanyevo! You're under arrest!"

When the man in civilian clothes made a move toward the lieutenant, Burhan quickly pushed his friend back into his chair.

"Dursun, this is not your problem. Just stay calm."

After Burhan slowly rose to his feet, Lieutenant Nihad frisked him for arms. He then ordered Burhan to walk in front of him. "If you try to run away," Nihad growled, "I'll shoot you. Let's go."

Dursun sat motionless as he watched Burhan led away by the Ottoman officer. Soon after they had left the coffeehouse, Dursun discreetly followed them. He wanted to know where Burhan was being taken. He watched Burhan and Lieutenant Nihad enter the command center of the Ottoman military at the end of the market street. He then returned to the coffeehouse, mounted one of Burhan's horses, and tied the reins of the other to the pommel of his saddle. He headed to the outskirts of Skopje where he was temporarily camped with the migrating Turkish villagers.

Upon arriving, Dursun handed Nurjahan the reins and told her in a hurry what had happened. He then ran to Selim's tent. As he caught his breath, he also tried to tell Selim what had happened.

Selim asked him to sit down. "My son," he said. "Stop talking until you've rested."

Dursun, after drinking a cup of water, told Selim all about the incident at the coffeehouse. "Very early this morning," he began hurriedly, "I went to town to check on the available travel possibilities to Anatolia. When I was looking for the transport station, I saw Burhan riding a horse through the streets. Even though he was in an Ottoman uniform, I recognized him just the same. He's the Albanian defector who saved our lives. I stopped him and asked what he was doing in Skopje. As he dismounted, he greeted me warmly. He had another horse with him, so we tied both horses to a nearby tree and went into a coffeehouse. As we sat down and began talking, an Ottoman officer, a lieutenant I think, came to our table, pointed his gun at Burhan's head, and arrested him. When they walked out of the coffeehouse, I followed them. The officer took him to the military command center. By the way, he told me that the day before he had brought a wounded Ottoman officer to Skopje. I'd like to help Burhan. If he's judged a traitor, he'll definitely be executed by the military authorities. What do you suggest we do now, Selim Baba? How can we help him?"

"My son, calm down," Selim replied reassuringly. "Let's see what we can do. I think we have only two options. First, we can talk to Servet Hanim to see if she can be of some help. Second, we could visit the nice lieutenant who was in charge of the military attachment to the hospital convoy from Yanyevo. I think his name is Nihad. You should tell him about your impressions of the young man who has been deemed a traitor. Let's go now and see Servet Hanim. Maybe she can help us meet Lieutenant Nihad."

Doomed

Lieutenant Nihad was summoned to the main office. He was told to sit and wait until the captain had finished questioning the prisoner. Half an hour later, two armed guards brought Burhan out of the interrogation room. His hands were tied behind his back. Burhan walked calmly past Nihad. Before leaving the room, he turned toward Nihad and asked him to speak with Lieutenant Avni. Without waiting for a response, he marched out of the room.

Nihad was perplexed, wondering what Avni had to do with this common traitor. He walked into the captain's office. After saluting his superior officer, he stood upright in front of his desk.

The captain put the document he was reading aside and told the lieutenant to take a seat. "You should prepare your deposition before the accused is tried in a military court this afternoon," he ordered. "I've decided that your reason for arresting him was justified.

The accused apparently was sent here by the Serbians to spy on our military situation. He'll be summarily judged and possibly condemned to death. He might be executed tomorrow morning. Write your report now. Give it to me as soon as you finish."

Nihad rose to his feet and saluted the captain. "Yes, sir," he replied. "You'll have my report on your desk within an hour." On his way out of the captain's office, Nihad wondered about Burhan's comment that he should have a talk with Avni. He promised himself that he would do so as soon as possible.

A Life to Spare

When the nurses wheeled Avni from the operating room, Servet was waiting in the hallway. She walked beside her husband who was still in great pain.

"Avni, how do you feel?" she asked.

"Not so well, but I'll be all right. Where's my little girl?"

"She's being looked after by good neighbors."

The nurses maneuvered the stretcher into the room. Inside, Avni recognized Jemal, who jumped to his feet with a smart salute. "Lieutenant!" he said loudly. "It's wonderful to see you again!"

"Jemal, I won't be able to say much now. Please accept my sincere gratitude for getting my family to safety."

A nurse carefully settled Avni into his bed. Servet sat on the edge of the mattress, and Jemal sat on the stool next to the bed. As Avni rested, Servet and Jemal had a quiet conversation.

"Jemal, how are you recovering from your wounds?" Servet asked. "What did the doctor say about the recurring infection in your shoulder?"

"He thinks I'll be all right," replied Jemal. "He says that I may fully recover in two or three weeks. Till now, I haven't heard from

Lieutenant Nihad about my release from the military. I hope he isn't going to take disciplinary action against me."

"Soon Avni will talk to Lieutenant Nihad about that matter. Would you like to know who saved Avni's life? Burhan, Mehmetali's renegade son, brought Avni to Skopje and delivered him to the hospital yesterday. Bless his heart; he took a tremendous risk by coming to Skopje. I hope he'll have a safe return to Yanyevo."

They spoke quietly about what Avni had told her of the Tepe Hills battle, about rescuing Mehmetali from the jail in Pristina, and about Mehmetali's unexpected death in Yanyevo.

There was a sudden knock on the door; Jemal stood up to answer. The guard at the door told him there were two men and a young woman at the guard station wanting to see Lieutenant Avni's wife. Servet overheard the conversation and asked Jemal to investigate.

Jemal went out with the guard. At the entrance to the hospital, he met Selim, Dursun, and Nurjahan. Selim gave Jemal a big hug and asked how well he was recovering. Selim then introduced Dursun and Nurjahan to Jemal. After a few minutes of discussion about why they had to speak with Servet, Jemal understood the situation. He convinced the guard to allow them to enter the waiting area to meet with the lieutenant's wife.

Servet was very happy to see Selim again. She told the old man that her husband had returned from the battle alive.

"Praise the Lord that your beloved husband is united with his family," replied Selim joyfully. "My respected daughter, allow me to introduce you to a couple of dear friends who need a special favor from you."

"My honored father, your friends are also my friends. Please, tell me how I can be of help."

Selim and Servet talked for a long time. When all was said, they realized that this meeting was the result of many unexplainable coincidences and intricacies of fate. They had been brought together to save the life of Burhan, to whom they all were somehow connected.

As he listened to Dursun's stories about Burhan, Selim realized that Burhan was the same person who had visited his village before their departure. Hearing Nurjahan's dramatic recounting of how Burhan had saved her life brought tears to Servet's eyes.

"I'll talk to both lieutenants," she promised. "God willing, they'll help this remarkable man. Please, come back to the hospital late this afternoon. I'll let you know where Burhan is and what's happening to him." Turning to Jemal, Servet continued, "Please, ask one of the guards where we can find Lieutenant Nihad. He should be informed that Lieutenant Avni urgently wishes to see him."

Lieutenants' Scheme

Jemal was surprised to see that Lieutenant Nihad appeared at the hospital not long after a soldier had been sent to fetch him. Jemal rushed to Avni's room. Lieutenant Avni was still asleep. Jemal quietly explained to Servet that Lieutenant Nihad was on his way up to meet Avni.

Servet nervously ushered Jemal to the door. "I don't think Lieutenant Nihad should see you," she said. "I'll welcome him. Please go to your quarters now."

They walked out of the room. Just as Jemal disappeared into one of the adjacent rooms, Lieutenant Nihad appeared from the stairs leading into the hallway. Servet stood in front of the door to welcome him.

Stopping in front of her, Nihad bowed cordially and asked her forgiveness for exposing her to misery and confusion with incorrect information about her husband's fate.

Without giving him a chance to continue with his apologies, Servet confidently remarked, "I accept your apologies, Lieutenant. I am so happy that you were wrong and Avni is alive and well."

"How is Lieutenant Avni doing? Is he recovering from his surgery?" asked Nihad.

"Yes, Lieutenant, he's recovering well. Unfortunately, you can't visit him now because he's resting. There's a serious issue he wanted to discuss with you. Maybe I could brief you about the problem."

As they stood in the doorway, Servet informed Nihad about Burhan in detail, describing his heroic efforts to save her husband's life. She also described the incidents involving Selim, Dursun, and Nurjahan.

Nihad responded solemnly, "Madam, while we're talking about Burhan here in the hospital, a military court is deciding his fate. Given the fact that he is an enemy soldier who was caught in Ottoman uniform here in Skopje, he'll definitely be condemned to death. There's nothing I can do about what is about to be decided by the military court. I'm sorry to inform you that he may be executed early tomorrow morning. Please, give my sincere apologies to Lieutenant Avni. Believe me, at this point, I can do nothing to change Burhan's fate. When I visit Lieutenant Avni tomorrow afternoon, I'll discuss the details of this issue with him. Please, excuse me; I've got to return to my office."

Servet was shocked by the lieutenant's blunt and insensitive response. She walked back into Avni's room and sat on the edge of the bed. Looking out of the window, she asked herself, "What are we going to do now?" *I've got to have an urgent talk with Avni before Selim and his friends come back here to see me. I've got to wake him up. He's the only one who can help us now.* She moved gently toward Avni and held his hand. She sweetly whispered into his ear that she loved him. With a serene smile on his face, he whispered back, "I love you, too." After a few moments of silence, she told him what was about to happen to Burhan. They discussed Burhan's unfortunate situation for a long time.

When a nurse came in to check on Avni, Jemal informed Servet that Selim was waiting for her down at the entrance to the hospital. Servet and Jemal went down to the hospital's reception area to meet Selim and his companions. They sat on wooden benches around a large table outside the main gate.

"Selim Baba," Servet began sadly, "I don't know what to do now. I informed my husband. He carefully listened to me, but he hasn't come up with a solution yet. I'm sure Avni will find a way to save the life of this young man. Otherwise, Burhan may face a firing squad tomorrow morning." Noticing tears in Nurjahan's eyes, Servet turned toward her. "You really care for him, don't you?" she asked. "Please, don't give up yet. We might still have a chance to save his life. Tonight, we should all pray for a miracle."

Later, when Servet and Jemal returned to Avni's room, they found him sitting on the edge of the bed.

"Servet," Avni said. "Will you and Jemal please help me get dressed?"

"Where are you going?" Servet asked abruptly. "You're in no shape to leave this room."

"I have to visit Nihad in his office," replied Avni. "I have to save Burhan's life. I owe it to him and to his father. Please, don't argue with me. Just help me get dressed." Turning to Jemal, he continued, "Go out and hire a horse-drawn buggy, then bring it to the hospital's entrance. Ask a guard to inform Lieutenant Nihad that I'm about to visit him. The lieutenant should wait for me in his office."

As he put on his jacket, Avni asked Servet to bring him a pen and paper.

"Are you planning to write a letter to Nihad?" asked Servet.

"Yes. Please hurry up," replied Avni.

The Twenty-First of January: The Firing Squad

The next day before dawn, Selim completed his usual morning prayers. He remained kneeling on his prayer rug for a long time, asking the Lord's compassion and mercy for Burhan. He finally arose and, donning his overcoat, went out from his tent into the cold morning air. Outside, next to the horses, Dursun and Nurjahan were waiting.

Dursun, his voice laden with sadness, greeted the old man, "Good morning, Selim Baba. We're coming with you."

All the way to Skopje, they rode side-by-side in silence. The city was beginning to wake up. The morning haze slowly dissolved as the sunlight gradually manifested over the skyline.

Hiding her face behind a scarf, Nurjahan commented. "What a beautiful day to die!"

Selim responded without looking at her. "Hush child! You have to believe in God's miracles."

They slowly wound their way through the empty, quiet streets of Skopje until they reached the Ottoman military training compound. They had been told that the military executions took place in the large marching arena behind the compound.

Tethering the horses to the fence post, Dursun remarked, "This is the closest we can get to the executions. Yesterday evening, I tried hard to meet Servet Hanim, but to no avail. I couldn't find her. Now we have no idea what is about to happen to Burhan. If he comes out with the condemned prisoners, he'll be shot. If he doesn't, then he has been saved. We'll soon know."

Selim sat cross-legged on the ground and leaned heavily against the fence post. He beckoned his companions closer to him and said, "Let's pray that he won't be among the condemned prisoners."

The Last Meal

Inside Burhan's cell, the prison guard handed him a plate of goat's cheese, dried black olives, and freshly baked bread. He said, in an unusually soft tone of voice, "This is a very good breakfast. In a short while, I'll bring you a cup of hot tea." After returning with the cup of tea, he mumbled, "Enjoy your last meal."

Burhan pushed the plate away. He held the cup with both palms to warm up his cold hands. As he sipped the sugary tea, Burhan spoke to himself. "What rotten luck I have! I should never have brought Lieutenant Avni to Skopje. Or at least I should have left the city immediately after delivering him to the hospital."

The previous night, he had not slept at all. Knowing his life would end in the early hours of the next day, he relived his childhood, his loving times with Katya, and the tragedy that had followed those good times. He thought, not too fondly, about the battles he had fought in the Serbian nationalist army. He could not remember how many people he had killed. "Too many!" he mumbled. "I'm not proud of it, but I had to do it." He wondered about Lieutenant Michailovitch. *Just like me, he is definitely in jail. However, unlike me, he is probably not awaiting his own execution.* The irony made him smile. *The lieutenant deserves worse,* Burhan mused, *but he's lucky!* He then whispered, "Nurjahan, it would have been nice to get to know you more." Suddenly remembering his father, he thought, *The only good part of this miserable predicament is that I'll be joining you soon, Father.*

He showed no reaction at all when Lieutenant Nihad entered his cell and stood silently in the middle of the room.

Suddenly, the lieutenant spoke. "Burhan, you and I must have a serious talk."

Burhan placed his empty cup on the floor and got to his feet. He turned his back on the lieutenant and walked toward the window. He did not want to listen to the man who was responsible for his approaching execution. Through the tiny window with broken glass, he felt the breeze and looked at the light blue sky. He suddenly felt at peace with himself. A sense of tranquility and complete submission to his fate overcame all his worries and fears. He calmly turned around and faced the lieutenant. "You are disturbing my peace of mind. What more do you want of me?" he asked sternly.

Lined Up to Die

Nurjahan recognized Burhan among the eight condemned prisoners entering the execution ground. She began to sob loudly. Selim and Dursun were also distraught, but they silently watched the procession of prisoners and marksmen. When Lieutenant Nihad came out of the administration building and entered the training arena, Selim instantly recognized him. He pointed him out to Dursun. "That's the lieutenant who led the convoy to Skopje," he said.

Dursun, who appeared highly agitated, loudly responded, "He's the man who condemned Burhan to death. He's a bastard!"

"Don't jump to quick conclusions, son. We don't know what happened yesterday. Maybe he tried but failed to save Burhan's life. We'll find out later."

Military guards lined up the eight condemned men two meters apart against the whitewashed stone wall. Eight marksmen took their positions facing the prisoners. Lieutenant Nihad briskly walked toward the marksmen, checking their positions, talking to each soldier and inspecting their loaded rifles. He then approached the prisoners and talked to each condemned man before they were blindfolded. Burhan was last one in the line of prisoners. He had a lengthy talk with Burhan before he was also blindfolded.

Lieutenant Nihad, taking wide, measured steps, marched toward the marksmen. Standing ramrod straight, he turned his face to look at the soldiers' profiles and ordered them to take aim. After a few heartbeats of silence, he loudly shouted, "Fire!" All the rifles simultaneously fired and the bullets hit their targets. With no expression on his face, Lieutenant Nihad calmly walked toward the wall. Before reaching the presumably dead prisoners, he took out his revolver. He checked the first man and then the second. When he reached the third man, he efficiently conducted a coup de grace. He continued to check the remaining men, including Burhan, who were all lying motionless on the ground. There was no further need for his revolver. As he placed it in the holster, he ordered the soldiers to carry the bodies to the burial area. He then strode purposefully away from the gruesome scene.

To Claim the Corpse

Nurjahan, nearly hysterical from what she had just witnessed, turned away from the execution scene. Wiping away the tears that were streaming down her face, she noticed Servet Hanim and a soldier pass them by on a cart. She pointed her out to Selim. "Is she here to claim the body?" Nurjahan asked.

"I guess so," Selim replied, "At least Lieutenant Avni was able to acquire permission to give Burhan a decent burial. Usually, condemned prisoners are buried in unmarked graves."

Slowly pulling himself to his feet, Dursun suggested, "Let's go and help her."

They formed a sad, slow procession and followed the horse-drawn cart as it approached the front of the military administration building. When the cart finally came to a jerky stop, Jemal jumped off and tied the reins to the iron post.

Servet calmly ordered Jemal, "Go in and have Burhan's body delivered to you. You're in no condition to carry the coffin yourself. Get a couple of soldiers to help you bring it out to the cart."

As Jemal disappeared into the building, Servet heard her name being called. She quickly spun around to see who was calling her.

"Selim Baba! How nice to see you," she responded. "Dursun and Nurjahan, what are you doing here?" Then, belatedly realizing why they were there, Servet apologized profusely for not being able to save Burhan's life.

"Servet, daughter," Selim said. "It's good that you have acquired the permission to give our friend a decent burial. We'd like to help you to find a proper graveyard for our dear departed friend. Where do you want to bury him?"

"I really don't know," answered Servet. "Is it possible to bury him in a cemetery near your camp?"

"Yes, by all means, let's do that. Should we help Jemal bring out the coffin?" asked Selim.

"No need, Selim Baba. Soldiers will help," replied Servet.

Jemal guided the soldiers as they carefully placed the wooden coffin onto the cart. He climbed up into the seat and smacked the horse's rear to get it moving. "Where are we going, Servet Hanim?" he asked innocently.

"To Selim Baba's camp, just as we decided this morning. Luckily, Selim Baba was here just a few minutes ago. He agreed to my proposal to bring Burhan's body to his camp."

"Where are they now?" asked Jemal.

"They've gone for their horses. They'll follow us."

A short while later, the horse-drawn cart carrying Servet, Jemal, and the coffin was joined by three riders with sullen faces. No one spoke until they reached the Turkish villagers' camp.

As she climbed down from the cart, Servet asked everyone to gather around the coffin to say a few prayers for the deceased. All five of Burhan's friends surrounded the coffin. As they got ready to pray, Servet suggested they take a last look at their departed friend.

"No, my daughter," Selim said. "We shouldn't do that."

As he reached out to remove the coffin's lid, Jemal asked, "Why not?"

Nurjahan turned her back to the coffin and started to pray in a voice filled with pain. Dursun commented that the last sight of their friend's bloodied body would not be a welcome memory. When Servet and Jemal lifted the lid, it was only Selim who had the courage to look into the coffin.

"Oh my Lord, he's alive! Burhan is alive!" shouted Selim.

With cries of disbelief and joy, everyone rushed forward to help Jemal untie Burhan's hands and feet. Selim removed the piece of cloth blindfolding Burhan.

Looking as pale as a dead man, Burhan, holding the sides of the coffin, slowly sat up. As he covered his forehead with both hands, he blinked repeatedly to adjust to the bright sunlight. Then, with a deep voice, he calmly said, "I'm alive! Thanks to you, my dear friends, I am still in this world."

Nurjahan shyly touched Selim's shoulder to get his attention. "One of God's miracles?" she asked cheerfully.

During the rest of this special day, the camp was full of excitement. The children played gleefully late into the evening while the camp dogs wandered freely around, tails up and high because that day no one felt like kicking a dog.

Just before sunset, Servet and Jemal rode back to town. They continued to talk about the amazing affairs of the day. Referring to Burhan and Nurjahan, Servet commented, "They look so nice together. Do you think they'll get married?"

"I wouldn't be surprised if they get married tomorrow. Servet Hanim, may I ask a question?"

"Sure, go ahead."

"How did Lieutenant Avni convince Lieutenant Nihad to become a part of this risky scheme to save Burhan's life?"

"Jemal, I really don't know. After he returned from his discussion with Nihad, all Avni told me was to go to the command center building with you the next morning and pick up Burhan's body in a coffin. When I expressed my disgust at what I thought was a cruel joke, he responded that Burhan would probably be alive inside the coffin. When I insisted that I deserve an explanation, he kept silent. This morning he promised that he would tell me one day how he did it. When he does, I'll write and share the story with you."

All's Well That Ends Well

Upon reaching Skopje in the evening, Servet rushed to the hospital to visit Avni. Sitting on the edge of the bed, she told Avni all that had happened. Starting with picking up the coffin for burial and finishing with the surprise ending at the Turkish villagers' camp, she dramatically recounted the intriguing events of the day. "You should have seen their faces when Burhan sat up in the coffin!" she said excitedly. "Sorrowful mourning became joyful celebration. Are you happy that you've saved the life of your friend's son?"

"Of course, I'm very happy to hear that our efforts spared Burhan's life. We did the only thing we could have done to save his life. I hope he'll stay out of trouble. Maybe he'll find a wife and settle down."

"That might happen sooner than you think," Servet said. Then she told Avni about Nurjahan. For the rest of the evening, they talked for a long time about all the amazing things that had happened in their lives during the last few weeks.

As he reached out to hold Servet's hand, Avni commented, "From the birth of our daughter to my survival on the battlefield, we were helped by many good people. Now, in return, we have been able to assist someone who needed our help."

Before leaving the hospital room for the residential compound, Servet asked Avni, "How much longer are you expected to stay in the hospital?"

"The doctor said two more weeks. Why do you ask?"

"I think I should visit my uncle in Yanya until you recover fully. During my visit, I'll get Bedia's birth certificate. Please, do Jemal a favor: ask Nihad to let him go home to his family."

"Don't worry!" replied Avni. "I'll take care of that matter, too. Unfortunately, Jemal's wife died a few months ago. Nihad decided not to tell him. I think Nihad will let Jemal go home in a week. Enjoy your family in Yanya. Please, return in two weeks. By then, we'll also know about my status in the military."

On her way out, Servet asked the guard to summon Jemal. After his arrival, they walked to the officer's compound. On the way, she told Jemal that Lieutenant Avni would soon resolve the discipline problem and that, within a few days, he would be on his way home to Sivas. When they reached the officer's compound, Servet brought Bedia outside. Having trouble finding the proper words to thank him enough for all he had done, she briefly uttered her farewell to Jemal. "My daughter and I owe you our lives. You will always be in our prayers. God be with you!"

Jemal took little Bedia in his arms. With tears in his eyes, he looked affectionately at Servet. "Servet Hanim," he said, "I'll never forget you and the lieutenant as long as I live. Please, remember to write me and let me know your whereabouts. Someday, let me know the real story of how Burhan's life was spared."

JOURNEY HOME

Early February 1910: Farewell to Friends

After searching the crowd for Lieutenant Nihad, who was late, Avni returned to the carriage to load their luggage. As he handed the last piece to the porter, he spoke to Servet.

"I think we could wait a few more minutes for Nihad. I just asked the carriage driver to delay our departure until he arrives. He's supposed to bring my travel documents. As soon as Nihad shows up, we'll leave."

Servet approached Selim who was holding Bedia in his arms. "It is truly a great honor that you came to say good-bye," she said affectionately. "Selim Baba, all the good news you've told us warmed my heart. It's wonderful that you've found a new homeland in Macedonia. I'm happy to hear that Dursun and his family decided to stay with you in your new village, and it brings joy to my heart to learn that Burhan and Nurjahan are getting married soon. I'm so sorry to miss their wedding. I truly wish I could be there to share this jubilant occasion. Please, tell them that we wish them a long and happy life together."

Selim handed Bedia back to her mother. "Servet, my daughter," he said cheerfully. "Have a safe journey home." The old man then gracefully reached out and touched Avni's shoulder. "You both will always have a home in our new village. Please, never forget that in our little village you'll always have friends who shared a wonderful journey of hope with you and your family. You'll remain in our prayers."

Shouting Avni's name as he ran through the crowd, Lieutenant Nihad finally reached the carriage. Gasping for breath, he greeted Servet and Selim, and handed an envelope to Avni.

"Here are your medical reports and travel documents. The senior staff at Skopje headquarters voted to recommend you for a medal of bravery and heroism. After reviewing your case, the military council in Istanbul may award you the medal."

Lieutenant Nihad, holding Avni's arm, continued, "My dear friend, it was a great personal honor for me to serve with you in Yanyevo. Like an older brother, you've taught me many important things. I'll always remember you for your patience and compassion. However, I want you to understand that I knew the letter you tried to blackmail me with was a fake. I realized that this case must have been incredibly important for you to attempt to deceive me. After careful consideration, I decided to help save Burhan's life on his own merit. But I must admit that you and your wife's efforts to save him convinced me to reconsider my earlier position."

With a friendly smile suffusing his face, Lieutenant Nihad saluted his comrade. After returning the salute, Avni stepped forward to enfold Nihad in a warm embrace. "I thank you for your support to my family during my absence," Avni said warmly. "I truly appreciate that you understood my intentions for saving the life of Mehmetali's son. If you ever pass by Izmit, please, visit us. Farewell, my friend, and God bless you."

On the Way to Salonika

In the carriage, Servet cuddled the sleeping Bedia and prepared to listen to Avni's explanation of how he had convinced Nihad to spare Burhan's life. Leaning back against the side of the carriage, Avni took a deep breath and began.

"Servet, do you remember that over a year ago I told you that Nihad had had some trouble with the local Croatian community? I never told you exactly what the problem was. On one of the days when I was the officer-in-charge in the absence of Colonel Husnu, Mehmetali asked me to meet a young local Croatian woman with a serious complaint against one of our officers. The Croatian woman came into my office looking very upset. She was a very pretty woman, probably in her mid-twenties. She told me that she had been having an affair with Lieutenant Nihad for the previous six months. After a long pause, she informed me that she was now pregnant. She handed me a written formal complaint against Nihad. The letter was very explicit, ending with an appeal for matrimony under the law. She was a widow; her husband had been killed during one of the attacks by the nationalist insurgents. After reading the letter, I asked Mehmetali to summon Nihad. When I informed Nihad about the complaint, his face turned crimson with embarrassment and anger. He knew he was in serious trouble. As I pointed at the letter of complaint on my desk, I asked him to explain his behavior. He pleaded with me to let him handle the matter privately. I left my office and asked her if she would agree to discuss her personal problem with Lieutenant Nihad before I took action on her complaint. She calmly agreed to have a talk with Nihad. I ordered Mehmetali to take the couple to an empty office next door. Before they left my room, I asked Nihad to let me know if they reached an agreement."

Servet, interrupting her husband, offered him a piece of homemade pastry. They ate their lunch silently, and as soon as they finished eating, Servet pleaded with Avni to continue the story.

"Over an hour later," Avni said, "Mehmetali came into my office and told me that the couple was ready to consult with me. The Croatian lady, after stating that she had agreed with Nihad's proposal, quietly left the office. After her departure, I asked Nihad to enlighten me about the details of his agreement with the Croatian lady. He informed me that he had agreed to give her three months of his salary, plus the cost of an abortion and the travel expenses to a Greek doctor in Skopje. He then asked me to destroy her written complaint. I told him I would destroy the letter, but only after he had delivered everything he had promised her. I was later informed that Nihad had kept all his promises."

Servet was overwhelmed by the story. She asked her husband, "What did you do with the letter?"

"What do you think I did with it?" replied Avni. "I destroyed it, of course."

"I don't understand," Servet responded curiously. "You had no evidence to use against Nihad. Without the evidence, how did you convince Nihad to help save Burhan's life?"

"It wasn't easy! Do you remember the night you asked me to help save Burhan's life? I asked you to get me a pen and some writing papers."

"Yes, I remember."

"That evening before calling on Nihad to discuss the matter," said Avni, "I reconstructed from memory the Croatian woman's letter of complaint. During our meeting, I showed Nihad the letter. He became very angry, and then he lapsed into a long silence."

"Wasn't he suspicious that the letter was forged?"

"At the time, I wasn't sure if he believed I had showed him the original letter. However, after a long pause, he agreed to find a way to save Burhan's life. We spent the rest of the evening scheming to keep Burhan alive. However, during his farewell to me a few hours ago, he told me he knew that the letter I had in my hand was not the original."

"Why did he do it, then?" asked Servet.

"He felt it was the right thing to do."

"Avni, before I went to the prison to pick up the coffin, you told me Burhan would be inside, hopefully alive. You warned me that he could also be inside the coffin and dead. You didn't want to tell me how the whole thing was arranged. Tell me now. How did he survive the firing squad?"

"I'll tell you. When Burhan received his last meal, Nihad went into his cell to explain our plan. Apparently, Nihad had a hard time making him listen. Finally, Burhan agreed to cooperate."

Avni helped Servet change the baby's diaper while he continued with the story.

"After talking to Burhan, Nihad went to the armory and gathered eight loaded rifles to be used by the firing squad. He removed the bullets from one of the rifles and marked the butt of the rifle. He then called one of his most trusted soldiers in the regiment and assigned him to the firing-squad. Nihad instructed the soldier to take the last position on the right, facing the prisoners. When the condemned prisoners were brought out to the field, Nihad ensured that Burhan was placed at the right end of the lineup, and discreetly reminded him to pretend to be dead after the rifles were fired. Later, he personally ensured that Burhan was transported to the burial room and placed in a coffin for delivery to Jemal. I remembered you saying that you wanted to take the coffin to Selim's camp. It was good that Selim was there to help you transporting and opening of the coffin. So that is the rest of the story. Now you know it all. It's a good ending, isn't it?"

"Yes, indeed. It was the very best ending for Burhan," replied Servet. "But I still wonder how he felt when he faced the firing squad."

Coming Home

The long and tiring carriage ride to Salonika took more than two days. During the journey, they reminisced about their time in Kosovo. Occasionally, in moments of silence, they admired the charming beauty of their little girl. Avni, not yet completely recovered from his surgery, did not complain about the arduous and painful ride. Servet, who was happy they had survived their ordeal, basked in her husband's company and had enjoyable conversations with Avni. As they traveled the winding, bumpy roads of eastern Macedonia, she had many interesting debates with her husband. During the silent periods, when Avni slept fitfully, she gazed at her baby girl and was overwhelmed by feelings of love and good fortune. She wondered what the future held for her and her precious family.

After a day of rest in Salonika, they took a two-day train ride to Istanbul. They arrived at the capital city of the Ottoman Empire early in the morning. After two long years in Kosovo, they were happy to be back in this beautiful and charming city. From the train station in Sirkeci, they took a carriage over Galata Bridge, across the Golden Horn. While passing the middle of the bridge, Avni, holding Bedia in his arms, directed Servet's attention to the hills of Galata where the Pera Palace Hotel was located. They reminisced for a moment, remembering their stay two years before at that wonderful hotel. Later in the afternoon, they took a short boat ride across the Bosphorus to the Haydar Pasha train station on the Asian side of the city. There, they boarded a train in the early afternoon. They traveled joyfully for the rest of the day and reached their hometown, Izmit, before sunset.

* * *

QUIETUS

July 1920: Escape From Izmit

In July 1920, the Greek army was quickly advancing into western Anatolia to conquer vast territories of the crumbling Ottoman Empire. Over the previous ten years, Avni and Servet had lived through two Balkan Wars and a world war. The long-lasting Ottoman dynasty was in its last throes of survival. The victorious allied armies of the Great War were occupying the lands of the defeated and disintegrating Turkish Empire. One warm July evening, as they were having their supper, Avni and Servet nervously discussed a plan to escape to Istanbul before the Greek army occupied Izmit.

In a desperate last-minute effort, Avni tried hard to convince Servet to leave immediately for Istanbul with the children to save their lives. Servet adamantly argued that leaving Izmit for Istanbul did not make any sense at all. She repeatedly asked Avni to explain why he believed they would be safer in Istanbul under the occupation of the British army than in Izmit under the occupation of the Greek army. She made her point by explaining that during her childhood her family had lived in peace for many years with the neighboring Greek families in the western Macedonia town of Yanya. She reminded Avni that she had spoken fluent Greek for many years and asked him if he could speak even one word of English. She already knew the answer.

Avni told her what he had heard from people who had escaped from the Greek-occupied areas in the Aegean provinces. He said that the Greek army treated the local Muslim population with relentless cruelty and persecution. He began to give details of the accounts he knew to be true. After hearing the horror stories of atrocities committed by Greek soldiers against the Muslim population in the Aegean region, Servet finally agreed to Avni's insistent request that they depart from Izmit before the enemy soldiers arrived.

The next morning, as he was leaving for his duty at the civil defense office in Izmit, Avni told Servet that she and the children should leave early in the afternoon that day, before the Greek army's expected arrival at the outskirts of Izmit. He told her that he would send a carriage by noon to transport them to Izmit's port. Servet promised her husband that she would be ready to leave the house. They agreed to meet at the entry to Izmit's port facility to take a boat to Istanbul together.

After Avni's departure, Servet hurriedly packed all her jewelry and a few valuables into a pouch and asked her oldest child, Bedia, to help prepare her four younger siblings for the journey. Bedia now ten years old, helped her mother and kept a watchful eye on her two rowdy brothers, Ilhami and Ikrami, aged eight and six. She also took care of her three-month-old infant sister, Veciha, and her three-and-a-half-year-old baby sister, Vedia. After four hours of frantic work, they were ready to leave the house.

As Servet carried the bags to the front porch, Bedia ran to her mother to inform her that there was a strange looking officer at the rear garden door. Servet rushed to the back of the house. When she opened the door to the garden, she came face-to-face with a Greek army officer. Servet calmly greeted the officer in Greek and asked him what he wanted. The officer, a junior lieutenant, was accompanied by a group of soldiers standing in an orderly manner in the backyard. He told Servet that his soldiers needed some food and water. He then abruptly elbowed the door open and entered the house. He saw Servet's children standing in the hallway and took notice of the pile of bags.

"Where are you planning to go, madam?" the Greek officer asked emphatically.

"We're leaving for Istanbul."

"You speak Greek very well. Where did you learn our language?"

"I was born in southwestern Macedonia."

As she told the Greek officer her background, she reached into one of her bags and pulled out a small leather pouch.

The Greek lieutenant grabbed Servet's arm and asked her to stop.

"Lieutenant," Servet calmly said. "I just would like to give you a present so that you'll let us leave." She opened the pouch to show him the gold bracelets that she had accumulated over the years as family heirlooms. "Please, let us go, Lieutenant," she pleaded.

A few minutes later, several Greek soldiers helped Servet and the children settle in a small boat docked at the shoreline near the house. She and Bedia began rowing the boat across the bay toward the port of Izmit.

"Mother," Bedia asked, "I thought Dad was going to send a carriage for us."

"Yes, he was supposed to do that, dear, but we couldn't wait for the carriage," replied Servet.

"Would those soldiers have hurt us if we had stayed?" Bedia further inquired.

"I don't know the answer, my smart daughter. Maybe they would have, maybe they wouldn't; but we couldn't take the risk. Do you know why they allowed us to leave?"

"No, I don't!"

"My beautiful daughter, they let us go because I spoke Greek and I gave them all of our gold."

Destination Istanbul

By late afternoon, the little boat with Servet, her five children, and a few bags reached the city's shoreline. They rushed to the port facility to find Avni, who was relieved to see his family safe and sound.

"I have been worried to death these last two hours," he complained. "The carriage left before noon to pick you up from the house. You were supposed to be here two hours ago."

Servet inquired, "Didn't the carriage return to Izmit?"

"Of course not! What do you mean?"

As they waited for the steamboat, Servet told Avni what had happened at their home across the bay. When Servet concluded her story, Avni commented, "Thank God the little boat was there for you to row across the bay."

An hour later, the news broke out that the Greek army would occupy Izmit the next day. There was absolute chaos in the port area. Avni and Servet struggled hard to get on the last boat leaving for Istanbul. At the entrance to the port, in order to get on the overcrowded boat, Servet had to give away her remaining pieces of jewelry, the two gold bracelets on her wrist.

The boat finally pulled away from the port of Izmit and headed for Istanbul. During the five-hour journey, Servet patiently listened to Avni's deep frustrations about the state of political affairs and the ongoing dismantling of the Ottoman Empire by victorious European powers. Avni told Servet with great sadness that since their marriage more than twelve years ago, they had put together a family while their country had completely disintegrated. Leaning shoulder to shoulder against the railing, they watched the slowly approaching night lights of Istanbul.

All of a sudden, as if whispering into thin air, Avni spoke. "The city we see in front of us used to be a center of power and authority. Now, it's only a crumbling ruin occupied by our enemies. I wonder what kind of future awaits us here."

Servet, holding her husband's hand, asked him to turn around and look at the wooden bench where their five children were gathered together. With a smile on her face, she replied, "My dear husband, they are our future."

October 1922: Soul Mates' Parting

More than two years later, during a cool October morning in 1922, Bedia, holding in her arms her younger sisters, Veciha and Vedia, entered her father's bedroom. She helped her sisters up onto the bed next to her father. Avni, with a great effort, sat up to greet his three daughters who were there to say good morning.

A few minutes later, Servet entered the room with a tray full of food and said, "The boys are on their way to school. They were running late, so they left without greeting you this morning. After school, they'll visit you."

Avni, gently stroking his youngest daughter's head, questioned Servet, "What's the news on the streets about the arrival of the Turkish nationalist army in Istanbul?"

"This morning, the next-door neighbor told me that the nationalist army is expected to enter Istanbul within a few days. The sultan has already left the country on a British warship. All of the remaining British forces are expected to leave the city soon."

"Oh, how sweet this news is to my ears," said Avni. "We will become a free country again. You know, Servet, since my first assignment at the eastern provinces just before we were married, fourteen years ago, we have seen our country fall apart, defeated and occupied, marking the end of our six-hundred-year-old empire. We have experienced it all. But now, there is new hope for our people. A new nation will rise from the ashes of the old empire. I wish I could be in the streets to welcome our victorious nationalist army to Istanbul."

Noticing the distress in her father's voice, Bedia quickly took the girls away. Servet sat next to her bedridden husband.

"Maybe we could go out together and watch the nationalist army enter the city. I'll find out exactly when and where the procession will take place."

"I wish I could do that, Servet," replied Avni. "It would mean a lot to me to see this special event. But as you know, I can hardly breathe. I have no strength to get on my feet. Please, will you take the boys to see this very special military procession? When you return home, you can tell me all about it."

Servet, her heart aching, reached over and gently stroked the face of her dying husband. With a broad smile, she said, "I'll certainly do that, and I'll describe every detail of the procession to you."

Three days later, the Turkish nationalist forces victoriously entered the former capital city of the now-defunct Ottoman Empire. A former Ottoman pasha, Mustafa Kemal, had led the Turkish nationalists in their defeat over the occupying armies of the European allies.

Servet and Bedia, with the two boys, aged eight and ten, happily watched the Turkish nationalist soldiers enter the city. After three long years of British occupation, the well-deserved liberation was a joyous occasion for the people of Istanbul. The victorious generals of the Turkish army, proudly riding on their horses, led the procession through the crowded streets. Servet and Bedia picked up the little boys and held them high so that they could see the warriors who had won the war of liberation. Not seeing Mustafa Kemal Pasha, the leader of the liberation army, among the generals, Servet asked the people around her. She learned that Mustafa Kemal had stayed behind in Ankara, the newly declared capital of the liberated areas of the former Ottoman Empire.

When they returned home in the early afternoon, they found Avni anxiously waiting for them. They sat around his bed and excitedly described the glorious procession of the nationalist army entering Istanbul. They talked long into the night. The children, noticing tears in their beloved father's eyes, were concerned. Avni told them that they were tears of joy and celebration.

Two weeks later, on one cold and rainy October evening, Lieutenant Avni passed away at the age of thirty-four from complications resulting from what was then called consumption.

EPILOGUE
KOSOVO
1999

September 1999: Leaving Kosovo

It was my last day in Pristina. Early that morning, I stood for a long time on the balcony of my sixth-floor hotel room in the United Nations compound, watching the city come alive. The main square and the streets leading up to it were crowded with all sorts of people. There were many NATO soldiers, who were fully armed, walking around or riding on armored vehicles, and the UN police force and project personnel were leaving the UN compound in droves to start their daily chores.

After spending two months in Kosovo, I felt that the bloody conflict of the last year had now been replaced by administrative and political chaos riddled with centuries-old ethnic rivalry. I realized that since the beginning of the twentieth century, many things had changed drastically in Pristina: the city had grown to become a sub-regional center in the Yugoslav Federation. However, all the physical and socioeconomic transformations that had occurred in the city over the past century had not been accompanied by similar alterations in peoples' minds. Centuries-old animosities and hatred between Muslim Albanians and Orthodox Christian Serbs remained unchanged.

Following an emotional farewell to the United Nations office personnel, Mohsen and I left Pristina for Skopje airport. As we rode slowly behind many armored vehicles and empty trucks on their way back to Macedonia, I stared at the hills where Yanyevo was located. During my stay in Kosovo, I had traveled extensively to many parts of the troubled province and deeply appreciated its natural beauty and charming people. My brief but substantial exposure to this unique land and its people gave me the opportunity to envision my grandparents' lives here in Kosovo at the beginning of the twentieth century.

As we slowly passed through the gentle plains of southern Kosovo, I thought about my grandfather's death at the young age of thirty-four. At the time of her father's death, my mother Bedia was almost thirteen years old. Circumstances compelled her to join the work-force to keep the family out of poverty. She left school and took a job at the local cigarette factory. She worked hard all her life to make sure that her family had a comfortable life and that her siblings and children could get the best possible education.

My maternal grandmother, Servet, lived thirty-two more years after the death of her soul mate, my grandfather Avni. Both of my grandparents' sons, Uncles Ilhami and Ikrami became officers in the modern Turkish military and raised lovely families. Both of my mother's younger sisters found suitable husbands and raised wonderful children.

On a beautiful spring afternoon in 1929, my mother Bedia met a charming young man of Albanian descent named Arif. Later, on a lovely autumn evening, she married this handsome and sensitive man. This loving union created me and my three siblings. All four of us now have many wonderful stories to tell our grandchildren.

The Future of Kosovars

Mohsen, as he pulled the handbrake, woke me from my dreamy contemplation. "Sir," he said, "we've reached the airport right on time. I will walk you through immigration."

"That is very nice of you, Mohsen."

"You know, sir, you're leaving a part of you in Kosovo," he declared warm-heartedly.

"That's true, Mohsen, but I'm taking with me what I discovered here -- wonderful memories of my grandparents."

As I reached to shake his hand good-bye, he gave me a bear hug. "My Albanian brother," he said. "Make time to write their story."

Before entering the airplane, I turned to look at the sky. It was a bright, clear day, much different from the high noon eclipse I had faced during my arrival two months before. A few minutes later, the plane took off on its way to Istanbul. As I watched the Balkan landscape thousands of meters below, I wondered about the political future of Kosovo. During the last week of my stay in Pristina, I had gotten the opportunity to talk with some prominent Kosovo Albanians and a few local Serbians who were trapped in the United Nations compound. The discussions I had with them gave me the feeling that there were no solutions to the historically determined political stalemate, save one: the extermination of one ethnic group by the other.

In Kosovo, the United Nations is presently enforcing a strategy to foster an integrated social system based on coexistence and cooperation. However, given the religious and ethnic fabric of Kosovo and its historical context, this strategy cannot be implemented successfully without the full cooperation and collaboration of the European Union.

It is a historical fact that there were continuous conflicts in the Balkans from 1909 to the end of the second Balkan War in 1913. It is also a recorded fact that during that period of time, Kosovo faced many major conflicts and minor skirmishes among Ottoman forces, Serbian nationalists, and Albanian insurgents who wanted to end the five-hundred-year-old Turkish domination of Kosovo.

As revealed in my story, Serbians came close to accomplishing their long-sought national goal in 1910. An important but ignored element of the struggle for Kosovo was the rightful claim of the local Albanians. Even though an independent Albania finally came into existence in 1912, it did not include Kosovo within its borders. The recent conflict in Kosovo between Serbians and Albanians was a natural outcome of the improper and unjust annexation of Kosovo by the Serbian state following the Balkan War of 1913.

As partly reflected in this family story, the Muslim population of southeastern Europe and the Balkans suffered continuous and relentless attacks, beginning with the Austro-Hungarian occupation of Bosnia and Herzegovina in 1878 and continuing until the end of World War I in 1918. Over that period of time, hundreds of Muslim villages and towns were destroyed, thousands of Muslims, including women and children, were killed, and many young Muslim women were raped. Most importantly, hundreds of thousands of Turkish, Albanian, and Eastern European Muslims were forced to emigrate to the Ottoman Empire, and, after its demise, into the Turkish Republic. Unfortunately during that time, neither the UNHCR (United Nations High Commission for Refugees) nor an effective global mass media existed to reveal and record the atrocities and crimes against the Muslim populations of Eastern Europe and the Balkan Peninsula. It is a great injustice that the European states' transgressions against the Muslims of Europe have continued into the twenty-first century, particularly in Bosnia, Croatia, Serbia, Kosovo, and Macedonia.

Fortunately now, thanks to the existence of the United Nations and the presence of an effective global mass media, the whole world is instantly informed of human rights violations against the Muslims of Europe. In this new century, peaceful resolutions to past and present injustices against the Muslims of Europe through fair and sensible policies are essential for the successful unification of Europe. If and when the members of the European Union abandon their outdated, awkward policies and improper attitudes toward non-Christian minorities, including Muslims, Jews, and Gypsies, there will be possibilities for peaceful settlements in Kosovo, Bosnia, Macedonia and other parts of former Yugoslavia and the Balkan Peninsula. Otherwise, the zealots of ethnic cleansing and religious purity will continue with their bloody struggle to destroy the dream of a truly civilized and unified Europe.

GLOSSARY OF TERMS

Anatolia .... : Asia Minor

Baba .... : Father; venerable man

Bey .... : Official title; Mr.

Divan .... : A sofa

Efendi .... : Mr.; gentleman

Fez .... : A tasseled hat worn by Ottoman men

Hanim .... : Lady; Mrs.

Harem .... : The women's section in a Muslim house

Hodja .... : Muslim priest

Kilim .... : A flat woven floor mat

Masjid .... : A small mosque

Mufti .... : A senior Muslim priest

Seraglio .... : Turkish royal palace

Shalvar .... : Baggy trousers

Sultan .... : Ruler; sovereign

Thrace............ : The peninsula in between the Black Sea and the Marmara Sea in southeastern Europe, which faces Asia Minor

Turban .... : Wrapped headgear worn by Ottoman men

Whirling dervish .. : A humble follower of the Mevlevi Sufi sect

Yagiz .... : Courageous

* * *

MAPS

MAP 1:
THE DECLINE OF THE OTTOMAN EMPIRE
[1699 - 1918]

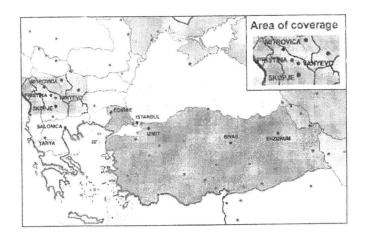

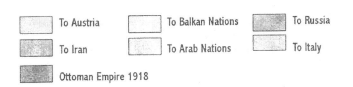

Ottoman Empire 1918

MAP 2:
OTTOMAN LAND CONCESSIONS IN EUROPE AND THE BALKANS

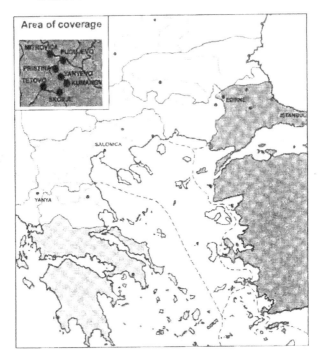

- To the end of the 18th Century
- To the middle of the 19th Century
- Between 1878 - 1913

MAP 3:
KOSOVO

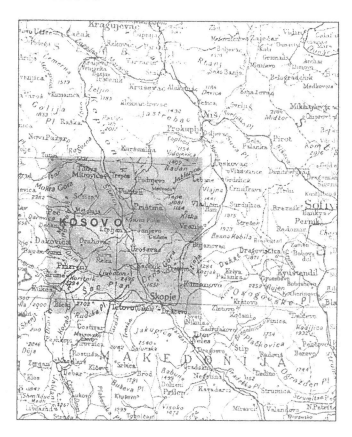

Area of Coverage in the Story

PHOTOS

Credits:
Photos 1 – 4 from the personal collection of Canerhan Tipi, Izmir, Turkey
Photos 5 – 8 from Omer Ertur's family collection

Muslim Refugees in Balkan Conflict c. 1912

Muslim Refugees in Balkan Conflict c. 1912

Turkish Prisoners Under Bulgarian Guard c. 1912

Muslim Refugees in Balkan Conflict c. 1912

Grandfather Avni (sitting on the right)
Military Academy - Istanbul, c. 1907

Grandparents Avni and Servet
Kosovo, c. 1910

Lieutenant Avni
Izmit, c. 1912

Grandmother Servet, Mother Bedia with Sister Sevim. (Mother is pregnant) Istanbul, c. 1935

ABOUT THE AUTHOR

OMER ERTUR was born and raised in Istanbul, Turkey. He received his education in the United States. He was professor of community and regional planning at Iowa State University in Ames, Iowa, and has lectured at various universities worldwide. As a planning and development professional, he worked with the United Nations and various international organizations, serving in Southeast Asia, the Middle East and Africa. In 1999, while working for the United Nations in Kosovo, he prepared the groundwork for a novel of his grandparents' life in 1910. In addition to various academic publications, he has completed three historical novels: *Farewell to Kosovo, A Prelude to Gallipoli,* and *Bones in the Nile.* The author, who has two children and a grandson, lives in Istanbul, Turkey, with his soul mate.

Made in the USA
Charleston, SC
03 December 2012